A Treasury of
Miracles for Friends

A Treasury of Miracles for Friends

True Stories of God's Presence Today

KAREN KINGSBURY

NEW YORK BOSTON NASHVILLE

FaithWords
Hachette Book Group
1290 Avenue of the Americas
New York, NY 10104

www.faithwords.com

Printed in the United States of America

RRD-C

First Edition: May 2004
Reissued: April 2015

10 9 8 7 6 5 4 3 2 1

FaithWords is a division of Hachette Book Group, Inc.
The FaithWords name and logo are trademarks of Hachette Book Group, Inc.

The Hachette Speakers Bureau provides a wide range of authors for speaking events. To find out more, go to www.hachettespeakersbureau.com or call (866) 376-6591.

The publisher is not responsible for websites (or their content) that are not owned by the publisher.

Book design by Giorgetta Bell McRee

Library of Congress Cataloging-in-Publication Data
Kingsbury, Karen.
    A treasury of miracles for friends : true stories of God's presence today /
Karen Kingsbury.
        p. cm.
    ISBN 978-0-446-53334-8
        1. Miracles—Anecdotes. 2. Friendship—Religious aspects—Christianity.
I. Title.
    BT97.3.K553 2004
    242—dc22

                                                                    2003024319

ISBN 978-1-4555-5885-8 (hc reissue)

To Donald, my knight, my prince charming,
my lover. My best friend. The miracle of your love and
light in my life will go on forever.

To Kelsey, Tyler, Sean, Josh, EJ, and Austin,
who have always believed us when we say that
your best friends are the people sitting around you
at the dinner table. Also to Thayne and Justin,
the newest additions to our family.

And to God Almighty, who has for now
blessed me with these.

Author's Note

It wasn't difficult putting together a collection of miracle stories involving friends, and I think I understand the reason why. Friendship itself is a miracle.

Friends.

Two souls striving to survive in the world, each with their own battles of faith, finances, and family; two souls wondering about love and life and loneliness, but who somehow together are stronger than apart.

Friendship knits together hearts and reassures us that everything will be okay, after all. The Bible says that two are better than one, that a friend is a strength in every sense of the word. Could a friend be anything but a gift from God? A miracle?

And so in exploring miracles involving friends, I was touched by the reality that friendship is often used by God to protect us, grow us, encourage us, and build up our faith. A friend will bring us laughter and camaraderie, compassion and understanding.

Sometimes that friend even brings us into God's territory—the place of miracles.

If you've journeyed with me through my other miracle collections, you know a few things about what lies on the pages ahead. Each story is inspired by a true event and then fictionalized for the purpose of this book. In each case, the miracle aspect of the story is true.

As you read, imagine the times when God has used a friend to bring about something miraculous in your own life. And be reminded that no matter how crazy and lonely and difficult life may be, we always have a friend in God.

Get ready to celebrate a treasury of miracles for friends! When you're finished, your heart will be forever encouraged.

A Treasury of
Miracles for Friends

The Most Friends of All

Larry Bradford was a social nobody at North Franklin High School.

Yes, he was active in his North Atlanta Christian Church youth group, a high achiever in his advanced academic classes, and the recipient of an Eagle award with the Boy Scouts. But his peers barely knew he was alive. Among the books he carried in his backpack was a leather-bound Bible, a gift from his best friend—his father.

"Why don't you have friends over once in a while?" his father would occasionally ask him.

"Because, Dad," Larry's gaze would drop. "The guys at school don't really like me. Not a lot, anyway."

Larry's dad would smile a crooked, sad sort of smile. "Well, son. Then that's what I'll pray for: That one day you'll have more friends than anyone in your class."

"Okay." Larry would grin and shrug his shoulders. His father was crazy to think anyone at Franklin High would ever connect with him, but that was okay. Friends at school didn't matter. Larry was different from the guys in his math and English classes, and he was okay with that. He had his dad, after all. Someone to talk to and pray with and fish alongside on the weekends.

His dad was all the friend he ever needed.

But when Larry was a junior in high school his father was watching a football game on TV when he suffered a fatal heart attack. The memorial service brought a scant fifty people—friends from church and a few close family members. A week later, the truth hit hard. Larry had lost his closest friend—and in his dad's absence, Larry's situation at school became clearer than ever.

He didn't have more friends than anyone in his class. He had fewer. Far fewer.

Thin and gangly, he was invisible, really. Not part of the preppy group or the social group, and definitely not part of the elite athletic group. At lunch he would sit by himself, reading his old leather Bible and wondering how he'd get through another day without his dad. Once in a while guys from one of the established groups would happen by and glance at Larry, sitting by himself with his ham sandwich and open Bible. Sometimes they'd whisper to each other, snickering and calling Larry a "Bible banger." Other times someone would sit across from him and ask a pointed question like, "What's the Bible say about hell?" or "How come you believe that stuff?"

"God's real. His truth is real," Larry would sometimes say. "What we believe about God doesn't change the truth."

The biting and hurtful comments from his peers didn't distract Larry. He was determined to become the man his father had been: faithful, devoted, a Christian with determination to live his life and one day raise his family in a way that pleased God. The way his father had raised him.

Larry finished school and walked for his diploma with dry eyes. He'd never connected with his classmates, so the transition from high school to college was not an emotional one. He attended college and graduate school, married a woman he met his junior year, and became a pediatrician. His wife gave him three daughters and a son, and Larry never regretted the friends he didn't have in high school. The only shadow of sorrow on the landscape of his happy life was the way he still missed his father.

On Larry's thirty-seventh birthday he received two pieces of mail—the first inviting him to his high-school twentieth reunion, the second confirming something his colleague and personal doctor had told him the day before: The flu-like symptoms he'd been experiencing for the past month were more than a weakened immune system.

He had a fast-moving, aggressive lung cancer.

"I have to be straight with you, Larry." His doctor raised an eyebrow. "We'll do everything we can on the medical side, but you know that prayer thing you always talk about? I'd get people praying right away."

Larry drew his family together, and he and his wife shared the news with their kids. "We're all going to pray for Daddy to get better," his wife said, tears spilling from her eyes. "And we're going to ask everyone we know to pray, too."

Early the next week, Larry shot an e-mail off to Robert Wills, their high-school class president and the organizer of the class reunion. The two had shared several classes together during high school, and Larry was certain Robert would remember him. Even if the two hadn't been good friends.

"Robert, I've been recently diagnosed with lung

cancer. I won't be attending the reunion. But if you could ask the class to pray, I'd appreciate it."

Robert received the e-mail and was cut to the heart. Larry Bradford? The good guy, the Bible reader? Stricken with lung cancer? Shaken, Robert sent an e-mail to the entire class explaining that Larry was a doctor now, married with four kids. And that he wouldn't be attending the reunion because he was battling lung cancer. He included Larry's e-mail address.

That's when the miracle began to play out.

One by one Larry began receiving e-mails from the members of his graduating class.

From the quarterback of the football team—a cocky, foul-mouthed kid—Larry received a note that read, "Larry, you were an inspiration to us all. This old world needs you, buddy. Hang in there, and yes—I'll be praying."

From a pretentious guy in his algebra class: "Larry, remember all those times you read your Bible and the rest of us didn't get it? Well, I get it today. I'm a Christian now, and I don't know—my whole life is different and maybe it's all because of you. Because you never backed down about your faith, not ever. You've got a friend here in Branson, Missouri, pal. A friend who'll be praying for you every day."

Larry was stunned by the responses. He shared them with his wife, his voice filled with awe. "You don't understand, honey. I didn't have a friend in school, not one."

"It's hard to believe," she said. "Look at what they're saying now."

Larry started treatment and a decision was made. He would have to have one of his lungs removed if he had any chance of survival. Surgery was scheduled for the following week. During his recovery in the hospital his wife brought him his laptop computer so he could check his e-mail.

Dozens of e-mails from former classmates filled the box.

"I got married three years out of high school and a year after that my wife left me," one guy wrote. "I was lost and alone, and I thought about ending it. But then I remembered you, Larry. Sitting by yourself every day eating lunch and reading your Bible. You had no one and you were so happy, man. I mean, always happy. It wasn't something that changed every day; it was part of who you were—a happiness that came from your eyes. That week, when I wasn't sure I could live another day, I bought a Bible and found a church. I've been a believer ever since. Fight hard, friend. You have no idea the difference you've made in my life."

Another said that she'd heard about the prayer rally of their classmates and had to get involved. In the process she'd reconnected with her best friend, someone she'd lost touch with a decade earlier. "We're both praying for you, Larry. You're bringing everyone together."

Against all odds, Larry began to improve. The reunion was two months away, and Robert Wills sent out another e-mail, this time to inform the class to keep praying for Larry's recovery—but to pray for something else, too.

"Pray he can come to the reunion," Robert wrote. "It's time we show Larry how many friends he has now."

And so they prayed.

Grown-ups who'd been a part of every social level at North Franklin High prayed alone and with their families and in online groups. They begged God to give Larry another lease on life, more time to grace the world with his unwavering faith.

"We need you, Larry," wrote a guy who'd been the partying type. "We all wanted to be like you back then. But only you had the guts to do your own thing.

You're our friend and our hero; you gotta make it, man."

Three weeks before the reunion, Larry was weak and struggling to maintain a positive attitude. But that day he received the best news he'd had since getting sick. The surgery appeared to have gotten all the cancer. Larry's radiation and chemotherapy sessions would be tapered off, and if things continued looking this well, they'd be discontinued.

"I didn't think you'd still be alive at this point," his doctor leveled with him. "Whatever you and your people are praying, keep it up."

"Have you thought about going to the reunion?" his wife asked him later that week. "They really want you to come."

Larry wasn't sure. He was touched beyond words by the outpouring from his former classmates, but he and his family lived in south Florida now, so it would mean a flight and several days away. He took his wife's hand. "Go with me?"

She smiled in a way that still melted his heart. "Definitely."

Larry continued to feel stronger, so they asked his mother to stay with their kids and they flew to Atlanta for the reunion. The night of the big event,

Larry had doubts. Sure he'd received e-mails that had touched him. But his class would still see him as the loner, the nobody. They probably wouldn't even recognize him, and with his health still a concern, he would've been better off staying home and spending time with his kids.

Before they walked out of the hotel and headed for the hall where the reunion was being held, Larry pulled away and prayed. "God, you allowed me to come here. Now let me make a difference for these people from my high-school days. Just let me make a difference."

They were half an hour late when they walked into the hall that night, and only then did Larry realize how many people were pulling for him. Robert Wills saw him first and motioned to a few others. Table by table the word spread, and people began smiling at him, standing, clapping.

A chill ran down Larry's spine, and he stopped short, staring at the outpouring. Beside him, his wife squeezed his hand and leaned close. "I thought you said you weren't popular."

Larry couldn't speak, couldn't answer.

In less than a minute, everyone in the room was on their feet, their applause filling the room.

"Larry! Larry! Larry!"

They chanted his name the way they'd once chanted for the school jocks. Robert came up to him and gave him a microphone. "Talk to 'em, Larry. Half of them wouldn't be here if it weren't for you."

"What do you mean?" Larry looked from Robert to his classmates, confused.

"I mean they wouldn't have come." Robert shook his head. "Everyone here's been praying for you, Larry. They came to see you, to thank you for showing them what it means to have faith."

The night was amazing, full of conversations Larry was sure he'd remember as long as he lived. The people who had shown him no concern back in high school now felt a shared sense of faith, a whisper of wonder that indeed God had granted them a miracle. Most special for Larry were the people who pulled him aside and apologized.

"I didn't understand you back in high school. But I do now," one man told him. "Faith is all that keeps me going. It's been a privilege praying for you these past weeks."

On the way home that night, Larry and his wife talked about all that had happened.

"It's a miracle." His wife shook her head, her eyes

brimming with tears. "The doctors didn't think you'd be here, and look at you."

Larry smiled, his grip tight on the steering wheel. "I would've had my miracle even if I hadn't been well enough to come to the reunion."

"Meaning?"

"Meaning twenty-three years ago my father prayed I'd have more friends than anyone in my class. I thought he was crazy." Larry chuckled, his voice tinged with awe. "But now look at me."

Note: Two years later, Larry died. One of his final statements to his wife was this: "I love you, honey. But just think . . . one day this week I'll get to see my dad again." The funeral service was a standing-room-only event, attended by his family, church friends, medical colleagues, and neighbors. And more than a hundred of his high-school classmates.

Double Miracle

Despite all the vivid reds and yellows in the tapestry of Tracy Black's life, one section was shadowy gray and darkest black. The part that represented her broken friendship with Anna Ritter.

Even though the split between her and Anna had happened five years ago, thoughts of her old friend still haunted Tracy, and that summer Saturday afternoon was no different. As Tracy worked in her garden, she wondered how Anna was doing, how her faith and family were. But mostly she wondered why Anna never called, how the two of them had let a friendship as golden as theirs fade away and die.

A sigh worked its way up from Tracy's soul. Thoughts about Anna never went anywhere. Anna had obviously moved on; it was time Tracy did the same. She picked another handful of beans and brushed a bit of fuzz from them. Other than the situation with Anna, life couldn't have been better. She and her husband, Paul, had three children and a beautiful home on three acres outside Akron, Ohio.

Tracy pulled another handful of green beans and dropped them in her bag. The kids were at a neighbor's pool, and Paul was working on the kitchen sink, so all around her the quiet was laced with only an occasional rustling of leaves or a buzzing bee.

I love being out here, God. Everything I see is something you made.

A sense of peace resonated within her and she smiled.

More handfuls of beans, and then a few of the bigger squashes. Tracy's bag was half full of vegetables when suddenly a sharp pain sliced through her stomach and she dropped to her knees. In all her life, Tracy had never felt anything so severe. She was only thirty-eight, a regular jogger who ate well and took care of herself. But the pain was so severe she could barely draw a breath.

"God...help me!" She could hear Paul's steps in the distance, hear the instant fear in his voice as he called her name and saw her huddled on the ground.

And in that moment she had a knowing, a sense that life as it had been was about to change forever.

Paul helped Tracy to her feet and to the hospital, where doctors gave her a shot for the pain. Their initial tests showed that she had a blocked intestine, and within the hour she was in emergency surgery to correct the problem.

When she woke up, her entire family was in the room. Her youngest son was ten-year-old Skyler. He approached her bed and took her hand. "I thought you were going to die, Mom." Skyler rubbed a fist across his cheek. The boy was an athlete, one who never cried about anything. But now his fears were obvious.

"Sweetheart." The thickness in Tracy's throat almost stopped her from saying anything else. "Everything's going to be fine. I'll be home in a few days, okay?"

Skyler nodded, his eyes still wide and damp. "Don't die, Mom. I need you."

Paul stepped up and put his arm around both Skyler and Tracy. Across the bed, the other two children stood quiet and somber. "Mom's right, she'll be home in a few days, guys. Everything's okay."

"Promise?" Skyler looked doubtful.

Tracy smiled despite the tears in her eyes. "Promise."

But the next morning the news was worse than anything they'd ever dreamed. The blockage had been caused by a tumor in her abdomen, a growth the size of a grapefruit that had cut off the intestine and caused the emergency.

"We're worried." Tracy's doctor pursed his lips and clutched his clipboard to his chest. "The preliminary tests don't look good."

Tracy stared at the man from her bed and tightened her grip on Paul's hand. What was he saying? Preliminary tests for what?

Paul was able to voice his questions first. "Are you thinking this . . . this tumor could be cancerous?"

Tracy's doctor nodded. "It looks that way. We should know more by tomorrow." He clenched his jaw. "I wanted you to be prepared. If we find cancer, Tracy will need extensive surgery and chemotherapy."

The entire time the doctor was speaking, only one thought screamed at Tracy—her promise to Skyler. This couldn't be happening. She couldn't be facing cancer and major surgery and death when she'd only the day before promised her youngest child that everything was okay, that she wouldn't die.

After the doctor left, Tracy and Paul held hands and prayed, asking God for a way out of the situation, begging him for a miracle. When they finished praying, they agreed not to tell the children until the next day when they had a definitive diagnosis.

"Take a nap," Paul told her as he left for home to be with the kids. "We have to believe God will work something out."

Tracy nodded and willed her heart rate to slow down. Fear wasn't from God, and Paul was right. She was exhausted. A nap would give her a way to pass the time until she knew for sure what her future might hold.

She fell asleep praying, and almost immediately she began to dream.

In the dream, she was crying and calling out to God, begging him to show her a way out of the tragedy that seemed about to befall her and her family. Then, in a clear and distinct voice, she heard God tell her what to do.

Have Anna come and pray.

Throughout the remainder of the dream, the thought stayed with her in a way Tracy couldn't shake. *Have Anna come and pray.*

When Tracy woke up, the notion was as strong

as it had been while she was sleeping. But now that she was clearheaded and awake, Tracy couldn't make even a little sense out of the thought. Have Anna come and pray? An ache settled in Tracy's heart; the idea was impossible. She and Anna hadn't spoken in five years.

But even as she argued the thought in her mind, she began to go back. Back in time to that place decades ago when she and Anna Ritter first became friends.

They'd been in history class together early in their freshman year when a boy in the farthest row tried to get Tracy's attention.

"Not now," Tracy hissed at him.

But the noise was enough to gain the teacher's attention. When he spun around and stared at Tracy, Anna shot her hand into the air. "I'm sorry, sir. I dropped my paper. Could you repeat that last sentence?"

The distraction worked, and Tracy avoided getting in trouble for talking. After class Tracy thanked Anna and the two giggled and chatted for several minutes. The next day they shared a smile and a certain knowing. A friendship had been forged.

From that day on Tracy and Anna became the

very best of friends, attending high school together and sharing details about every date and dance and struggle until they graduated. The two were separated for a few years when Anna went away to college, but afterwards, they each married and settled a few miles away from each other outside Akron. They shared in each other's weddings and the birth of each other's babies. Before their children were in school, they took five years' worth of walks at the local high school, picnics at the parks, and trips to the library. Again time moved on, and Tracy and Anna shared the trials and triumphs of raising school-aged children.

It was a friendship both women thought would last a liftetime.

But then one late spring afternoon Anna came to Tracy for a small loan. Their family van had given out and they needed a new vehicle, but with Anna's husband between jobs, borrowing money from a bank was not possible.

Tracy, meanwhile, was married to a man who brought in an annual income of nearly seven figures. They were generous with the money God had blessed them with, willing to help anyone in trouble. Because of her friend's obvious need, Tracy checked with her husband and easily agreed to help.

"I hate borrowing from you," Anna told Tracy. "But we'll have income in a month. After that we can make payments."

Tracy smiled and took her friend's hand. "I'm not worried about it. Pay it back when you can."

The loan was for five thousand dollars, and with it Anna and her husband, Ken, bought a used van that allowed Ken to take a job in downtown Akron, one that paid even better than the one he had lost.

Finally, five months after loaning the money to Anna and Ken, Tracy and Paul made plans to have their friends over for dinner. It was the moment they had chosen to discuss with Anna and Ken a payment plan for the funds they'd borrowed.

It was October, and a chill hung in the air as Anna and Ken arrived that evening, smiling and quick with their happy greetings. "I wouldn't miss Tracy's lasagna for anything." Ken patted Paul on the back and grinned.

The small talk continued while Tracy marveled at the situation. *They have no idea we're going to ask about the money,* she thought.

When dinner was over and the dishes cleared, Tracy made coffee and the four sat in the living room.

This was the moment, and Tracy prayed silently that the issue could be brought up and dealt with quickly, without any tension or hard feelings.

"Listen," Paul started. He sat back in his chair, his features calm and relaxed. "You remember that loan for five thousand dollars." He hesitated and looked at Tracy. "Tracy and I were wondering if this would be a good time to set up a payment plan."

Anna and Ken exchanged a strange look, and Anna cleared her throat. She kept her eyes away from Tracy, focusing instead on only Paul. "What loan?"

What happened next was something Tracy thought about often. The conversation turned stilted and tense, and Anna refused to look at Tracy even once. Ken denied knowing anything about the loan. Finally he snapped at Paul that yes, he would pay the money back, but their friendship would never be the same again.

After the couple was gone, Tracy stood frozen in place, staring at the front door. "What just happened?"

Paul came up beside her. "I have no idea."

They rehashed the conversation, the details of the loan, the attitude Ken seemed to have, the strange, furtive glances from Anna, and they decided on one

thing: There had to be a mistake somewhere. Before turning in that night, again the two prayed that God would help Anna and Ken see the issue more clearly and that the matter could be resolved without damaging their friendship.

But when two weeks passed without word from either of their friends, Paul called Ken and talked over the situation on the phone. Ken reluctantly agreed to pay the money back, with two-hundred-dollar payments starting the following Friday.

Tracy wasn't surprised when that Friday came and went without either payment or word from Anna or Ken. Another two weeks went by and finally Tracy and Paul agreed to forget about the loan and call it a gift. Their own family didn't need the money, and if that would prevent a rift between the two couples, so be it.

Tracy called Anna to tell her the news.

"Look." Tears gathered in Tracy's eyes and her voice trembled. "We've been friends forever, Anna. We can't let money ruin things." She paused. "Paul and I have decided to make the loan a gift."

"Meaning what?" Anna's voice was cold, distant.

"Meaning you owe us nothing."

For a while neither of them said anything. Then

Anna voiced a curt thank you and the conversation ended.

Weeks became months after that. Occasionally Tracy would call Anna, asking her out to lunch or over for coffee. But always Anna had an excuse. One afternoon nearly a year after Tracy and Paul had given them the money, Anna returned Tracy's call and stated the situation in terms that cut Tracy to the heart.

"It's over, Tracy. Ken feels awkward when the two of us talk." She was quiet and it was impossible to tell if she was crying or not. "It's time to go our own ways."

Tracy was in shock for hours after the phone call, stunned and angry and filled with sorrow all at the same time. Memories filled her mind of times when she and Anna had been closer than sisters. Now all of it was gone for reasons that didn't even make sense.

That had been five years ago.

The images faded and Tracy looked around her hospital room. She hadn't heard from Anna once in the past several years, and though the ache of losing her friend had never quite gone away, she could do nothing about the loss.

So why now, in her most dire hour, did she feel so prompted to call Anna?

She closed her eyes and prayed. *Lord, surely it's not you telling me to call her, right? Anna wants nothing to do with me.*

Yes, daughter. Make the call. Anna needs to pray for you.

The thought shouted into the hallways of her heart as clearly as if someone had spoken the words out loud in her room. A chill passed down Tracy's arms and legs. Anna needs to pray for me? The thought seemed outrageous, but Tracy had made a habit of heeding such thoughts. Especially if they were persistent even after she prayed.

Without giving the matter any more thought, she picked up the phone and dialed a number she still carried in her memory. Seconds later Anna's voice sounded on the other end.

"Hello?"

The sound of her friend's voice brought back another thousand memories.

"Anna? This is..." Tracy tried to finish her sentence, but she couldn't. Tears choked off her words and she pressed the receiver to her shoulder while she fought for control. When she was able to talk, she lifted the phone and said, "This is Tracy. I'm in the hospital and I'm sick, and...and I think God wants me to ask you to come pray for me."

At first Anna said nothing. Then in a voice strangled with its own emotions, Anna spoke. "I'll be right there."

An hour later, Anna walked through the door of the hospital room and years of silence and differences faded away in an instant. Anna came to Tracy, sat on the edge of her bed, and the two hugged as they hadn't in a long time.

"I'm sorry, Tracy, I didn't know what else to do." Anna was crying, letting her tears soak into Tracy's hospital gown. "Ken and I..." Her voice trailed off. "Ken left me a year ago."

The shock was one more in a series that afternoon. Anna and Ken had been churchgoers, people whose faith should have kept them together. But the announcement gave Tracy insight into the death of their friendship. They talked more about what had happened during that awful time five years ago, and after an hour, the air between them was clear once more.

"You wanted me to pray?" Anna had moved onto

the chair beside Tracy's bed. "What's wrong, Tracy? How sick are you?"

Tracy's heart sank as she considered the news from earlier that day. "They think I have cancer." She placed her hand over her abdomen. "I have a tumor here the size of a grapefruit. I'll know more tomorrow." A sad smile lifted the corners of her mouth. "I had a dream and God told me to call you. He wanted you to pray."

Anna nodded and placed her hand over the area where Tracy's tumor was. "God, my dearest friend needs a miracle. Please remove the tumor from her body and make her well again." Anna's voice cracked. "You see, Lord, I've been sick for five years, sick in my heart over the loss of Tracy. And now... now I'm healed. So please...do the same thing for Tracy."

After the prayer, the two talked for another hour, and then Anna left with promises to call the next day. "I'm not letting you go again," Anna said as she walked toward the door of Tracy's hospital room. "I believe tomorrow the doctors will find that a miracle has happened."

The next day, Paul arrived early. He was stunned by the news of Anna's visit and prayer time, the way the two had reconciled. But when the doctor came in, Tracy could tell immediately the news wasn't good.

"It looks like an aggressive type of cancer." He bit the inside of his cheek. "We need to take more tests today to determine the borders of the tumor and how fast it's growing."

The blow was more than Tracy had imagined. All night she had clung to Anna's parting words— that God might work a miracle and heal her. Now, though, she'd been handed what was likely a death sentence. And that meant she wouldn't be able to keep her promise to Skyler.

Tests were done that morning, and two hours later the doctor was back again. He entered the room with a strange look on his face and set a file of notes on Tracy's bedside.

"Well?" Paul squeezed Tracy's hand, his face ashen as he waited for the news.

"Just a minute." The doctor pulled the sheet back from Tracy's midsection and through her gown carefully felt her abdomen. The exam seemed to go on forever, until he finally straightened and stared first at Tracy, then at Paul. "It's gone."

His words didn't sink in immediately.

"What do you mean?" Paul's tone held a stunned quiet.

The doctor looked at Tracy. "I mean the tests showed absolutely no signs of the tumor." He motioned to Tracy's abdomen. "I'm feeling the same place where the tumor existed just yesterday, but today I feel nothing at all." His eyebrows came together and lowered, confusion written in the lines on his face. "It's completely gone."

A giddy sensation coursed through Tracy. She sat up in bed and looked at Paul. "Anna prayed this would happen. God told me to call her here so she could pray, and she prayed for this exactly."

The doctor took a step back and shrugged. "I'd like to run more tests tomorrow before you go home." He shook his head. "Tumors that size don't just disappear."

"They do when God wants them to." Tracy's heart swelled within her at the miracle God had given them.

The next day the news didn't change. The tumor was gone, her tests were normal, and that afternoon Tracy went home to a welcome that included Anna and her children. When the two friends had a moment alone, Tracy thanked her for having the faith to pray for a miracle.

"We were both healed," Anna said. "You of your tumor and me of my guilt and shame." Her eyes shone. "God didn't give us one miracle, he gave us two. First, that you're here..."

Tracy hugged her friend once more and then searched her face. "And the second, that you're here."

Buckle Up

❧

Andy Conner grabbed an apple and headed for the front door just as his mother came down the stairs. Andy and his best friend, Jared, were interns for the Birmingham, Alabama, firehouse, and that night they faced four hours of drills. Jared was waiting for him outside, since the two had just twenty minutes to get to the station.

"Fire drills again?" His mother leaned against the railing and smiled at him.

"Yep." Andy took a few steps out of his way and gave her a quick kiss on the cheek. "See you around midnight."

"Be safe." Her eyes met his and held for a moment. It was something she said often, especially since Andy's father had died of a stroke a year earlier. Now it was just Andy and his mother, and she wasn't excited about his decision to be a firefighter.

"I'm always safe." He grinned at her and took a few steps toward the door. "That's my job, Mom, remember?"

She let her gaze fall to the carpet and muttered, "Because of Jared."

Andy stared at her. "What?" The sound of a car honking came from outside and Andy knew they'd be late if he didn't hurry. Still, he wanted an explanation for his mother's words. His tone grew tight and harsh. "I'm not in this because of Jared. I'm in it for me."

His mother angled her head and looked at him again. "Please, Andy, be real. Since third grade you've done everything that boy's ever done. Baseball . . . target shooting . . . fishing. If Jared did it, you did, too."

Andy had turned nineteen that fall, and his mother's words grated on him. "I'm my own person, Mom. If I happen to like the same kind of work as Jared, it doesn't mean I can't think for myself."

The car outside honked again and Andy gave up the fight. He spun around, shook his head, and headed for the door.

"Andy, don't leave like that. I was only—"

Andy walked out and shut the door. Being patient with his mother was getting more difficult all the time. Yes, she was lonely, and since he was all she had left, she worried about him. Andy understood that. But couldn't she see how much he enjoyed working for the fire department? Why couldn't she be happy for him instead of making him feel as if his entire existence was directed by Jared?

Andy narrowed his eyes as he climbed into the passenger side of Jared's car and slammed the door behind him. Jared backed the car out of the driveway and sped off toward the station. It was fourteen miles away on a winding two-lane road and they'd have to push it if they were going to be on time.

A minute into the ride, Jared turned to Andy and raised an eyebrow. "Bad day?"

Andy leaned his head back and raked his fingers through his hair. "My mom won't give up."

"Your dad?" Jared kept his eyes on the road as he turned left and entered the two-lane leg of the drive.

"Yeah. Same story. She wants me to stay home in a glass bubble." Andy tossed his hands in the air. "She's trying everything to change my mind about firefighting."

An easy silence settled between them. Andy stared out the side window and thought about his mother's statement. Was that really how she saw it? That he'd done everything Jared had ever done? He gritted his teeth and gave a slight roll of his eyes. Things hadn't been that way at all. But if that was how his mother saw his friendship with Jared, maybe that was how everyone saw it.

Even Jared.

Andy had prayed more since his father's death. The time in conversation with God made him feel as if he had a dad to talk to again, and now, as they made their way to the fire station, Andy did just that. *God, help me be my own man. Please, God . . .*

Usually when he prayed, he felt some sort of reassurance, a sense that God was right there whispering some kind of answer. But this time, with his heart angry and frustrated, he felt nothing from God. No response at all.

Beth Conner stared at the front door for a moment before making her way into the living room, dropping onto the nearest sofa, and staring out the front window. She pressed herself into the sofa back and folded her arms as the taillights of Jared's car disappeared down the street.

Why did he have to get so mad?

Now he'd be gone the entire night, possibly fighting a deadly fire, and they hadn't even parted on good terms. She hated that he wanted to be a firefighter. A friend of hers had lost her husband, a firefighter, in the collapse of the World Trade Center. Since then Beth had been even more aware of the dangers of the job. It seemed a fireman was always being killed in one kind of tragedy or another. The very thought of Andy in a burning building paralyzed her with fear.

Why in the world would Andy want a job so dangerous?

The answer was obvious. Jared. Andy hadn't mentioned firefighting once until Jared took up an interest in it. No matter what Andy wanted to tell her, she was right about the fact that Andy looked up to Jared. Andy was a year younger, and since the two of them met in grade school, Andy had been Jared's tag-along pal.

That wasn't always a bad thing, but it wasn't always good, either.

Her eyes fell out of focus and she thought back through the years. The time when the boys had been ten and eleven and they'd tossed rocks against the bedroom window of the girl across the street. That had been Jared's idea, hadn't it? And when one of the rocks broke the window, Jared had been the first to flee the scene. Of course, both boys took equal punishment for it, but Beth began to doubt the benefit of Jared's role in Andy's life.

The two had been in mischief again after that.

When they were thirteen and fourteen, Jared had grabbed the keys to his father's pickup and taken Andy for a joyride through a local farmer's field. Beth could still remember talking to Andy about that event.

"Why, son? Why did you get in the car?"

"Mom..." Andy had shrugged, his face blank. "I couldn't let Jared go alone."

For the most part, Beth had merely tolerated Jared's role in Andy's life. She closed her eyes. *If only I'd broken up their friendship all those years ago, Andy wouldn't be pursuing such a dangerous job...*

She blinked and the images from the past disappeared. The reason they'd stayed close was because of Joe. Her husband had been happy and upbeat until the day he died, and his attitude about Jared had always been positive.

"He's a kid, Beth," Joe had always told her. "Of course they're going to get in some trouble. But he's a good boy. I think in the long run Jared will be good for Andy."

Beth wanted to believe Joe, even now. Firefighting, after all, was not a bad thing. But it wasn't safe, and the idea that Andy had gotten into it after Jared only convinced her that the older boy was still leading Andy into places where she didn't want him to go.

She looked out the window again and exhaled hard. What was this feeling strangling her heart? For a moment she considered her feelings, the frustration and suspicion and, yes, meanness she exuded so often. Then her eyes shifted and she saw the Bible sitting on the table.

God, why can't I let Andy go? And how come I can't learn to like Jared? The situation keeps coming between me and Andy. God, I need your help. She felt the sting of tears in her eyes. *Otherwise Andy's going to hate me.*

For a long while she waited, and then slowly, bit by bit, a feeling began to surface in her heart. She needed to give up her way of thinking in both areas. First, she needed to give Andy back to God.

"I can't keep him safe, God." She whispered the words into the empty room. "So you take care of him. That way I won't have to worry."

Second, she needed to believe that her dead husband had been right. Jared was loyal to Andy, and the two had certainly done as much good together as they had bad. Beth bit the inside of her lip and looked out the window to the dark sky beyond. "Okay, God, fine." Her voice still barely audible, she pictured the two boys. "Help me love Jared. Help me appreciate his friendship for Andy. And help me see it as a good thing in my son's life."

The boys were halfway to the fire department when Jared turned to Andy and chuckled. "You must really be mad at her."

"I guess." Andy leaned against the passenger door and studied his friend. "She said some rotten things."

"Wanna talk about it?"

"No." Andy glanced at the road in front of them. He would never let Jared know his mother's feelings, that she didn't think him a good friend. Andy managed a smile. "No big deal. Same old story, you know? Too protective; won't let go. That kind of thing."

Jared nodded, but as he did, he glanced down at Andy and his face fell. "Hey, man, put your belt on. Remember the rule?"

Andy remembered. The rule was something specific to their fire station, and it played over in his mind: *Firefighters show the way; buckle up every day.* It was a good rule. Not that it really mattered. The odds of a wreck were one in a million, right? He caught Jared's eye and saw that his friend was still watching him.

"Come on, buckle up." With his chin, Jared motioned to Andy.

Andy was about to reach for the belt when a thought hit him. This was just what his mother had accused him of, wasn't it? Always doing whatever Jared suggested? He'd never been much for seatbelts in the past, and who cared about the guys at the fire station. Half of them probably didn't buckle up, either.

But here he was, ready to do it simply because Jared told him to.

He let his hand settle back on his lap and leaned against the door once more. "I don't like seatbelts."

For a few moments, Jared said nothing to challenge him. Then he told him something he'd never said before. "You know something, Andy? All my life I've been lucky to be your friend."

"You've been lucky?" The statement caught Andy off guard. He leaned forward. "What's that supposed to mean?"

"I've been lucky. Things haven't usually been great at home, what with my mom divorced and dating all the time. But always, man…" He glanced at Andy again. "Always I have you." He glanced at Andy's seatbelt. "So buckle it, okay? I need you around."

Something in Jared's tone was strange, more urgent

than usual. Neither of them had worn seatbelts before working for the fire station, and never once had Jared been so insistent. Once more, Andy thought of his prayer, the way he'd asked God to help him be independent. But maybe this was different. He thought for a moment more and then shrugged. It didn't make him a mindless follower if he buckled his seatbelt, did it? Besides, how often had Jared come straight out and asked him to do something?

"Fine." Andy gave an exaggerated huff and flashed a tired grin at Jared. He reached over, grabbed the buckle, and snapped it into place.

At the same instant, he heard Jared scream, "Look out!"

Andy never saw it coming. A flash of something metallic filled the windshield and then he was suddenly spinning, his senses consumed with the sound of screeching tires, shattering glass, and twisting metal. Not until the sickening noise and jarring motion finally stopped did Andy realize what had happened.

They'd been in an accident.

The car had gone off the road and hit a tree. Now dust filled the compartment and broken glass covered his legs, but Andy was alive. He shot a quick look at

Jared beside him and saw that his friend was awake, his eyes wide. Blood dripped down his hand, but otherwise he looked unhurt.

"Can you believe that?" Jared was breathless, shocked.

An understanding began to dawn in Andy's heart. Everything had happened too fast for him to recognize the truth until now. Seconds after Jared had asked him to buckle up, they'd been in an accident. Seconds.

The doors were too jammed to open, so Andy and Jared waited until paramedics and firefighters from their own station arrived on the scene. Only then did Andy know for sure that his friend's advice had been nothing short of a miracle. A miracle that had saved his life.

One of the firefighters explained what had happened. According to witnesses, a truck had swerved into Jared's lane, causing Jared to jerk the steering wheel. The sudden jolt sent the car careening off the roadway straight into a tree.

"Good thing you had your belts on," the fireman said. "An impact like that and you'd have been dead instantly. Straight through the windshield into the tree."

*　　*　　*

Beth got the call from the hospital an hour later. Andy explained the situation, how the two of them had been driving along when for no understandable reason, Jared insisted he use his seatbelt.

"I thought about what you said, Mom. How I have to do everything Jared does. And you know what?" Andy's voice still sounded shaken. "I almost didn't use it because of that. But then Jared told me he needed me as a friend, that he didn't want anything to happen to me, and that's when I decided to buckle up."

Beth's hands began to tremble at the news, and long after the phone call was over she could only sit at the kitchen table and stare at her fingers. God had worked a miracle; otherwise Andy wouldn't be alive. By criticizing her son's friendship with Jared, she had almost killed him.

Then, as the reality of the situation sank in, she realized that Jared's strange timing had also been an answer to her own prayer. First, that she let go of her son and trust him to God. And second, that she might learn to see Andy's friendship with Jared as a good thing. The same way her husband had always seen it.

Now, in a single event that had saved Andy's life, both prayers had been answered in an instant. And as Beth found her purse and keys and headed for the hospital, she knew what she wanted to do the moment the boys were released.

Take Jared in her arms and thank him.

Returning the Favor

Rob Garrett could hardly believe how quickly his life had fallen apart.

One month, he and his wife and daughters were happy and healthy, living in a dreamy part of Thousand Oaks, California, where they were involved in their church and every day seemed better than the last.

Then, just after Christmas, the Garretts' youngest daughter, six-year-old Alicia, came down with a series of unexplained fevers. Two weeks of doctor visits gave them nothing to go on, no diagnosis. About that time, Alicia began bruising. Nothing that seemed out of the ordinary at first, just a bruised knee or a mark on her arm. But when the bruising got worse, Rob and his wife took Alicia back to the doctor's office.

This time the doctor ran a series of blood tests. The news was worse than anything they'd imagined.

Alicia had leukemia.

"I'm afraid it's advancing quickly," the doctor told them. "She'll need a bone marrow transplant very soon."

Rob could barely feel his heartbeat as he listened to the news. It wasn't possible. His brown-eyed little girl couldn't have gotten so sick in so short a time. He forced himself to concentrate. "How soon, doctor?"

"Within a month." The doctor looked from Rob to his wife and back again. "We'll test your family members first, but if there's no match there, then I'd say it's time for drastic measures."

Rob was on his feet, anxious to find Alicia and take her into his arms, desperate to love away her sickness. He studied the doctor one last time. "Drastic measures?"

"Yes." The doctor shoved his hands into the pockets of his white coat. "Time to pray for a miracle."

In Fort Wayne, Indiana, some two thousand miles away, Peter Hickman could barely get over how well his life was going. He was the president of a major division of a nationally known biotech company and married to the woman of his dreams, with two children—a boy and a girl.

He wasn't a praying man, but lately he'd taken to thanking God and asking for just one thing: That he might find the man who had made his wonderful life possible.

That man was Rob Garrett.

Thirteen years earlier Peter had been the least popular boy at St. Thomas High School in Detroit, Michigan. St. Thomas was a private school with fewer than a hundred students making up each grade level. But among those, Peter had the least number of friends. Back then he wore tortoise-shell glasses and his clothes hung on his small frame. He loved math and history classes, but when he tried to discuss algebraic theories with his classmates, they only laughed and looked the other way.

For the most part, Peter was used to living as an outcast on campus. But one girl—Maryanne Ellis— had captured his heart from the first day of school. She wasn't too tall, but she had blonde hair halfway to her waist and blue eyes that caught the sun. Peter was sure she was the prettiest girl he'd ever seen. But he was just as sure she'd never notice him, never know he was alive.

Then one winter day in his American history class, he felt a tap on his shoulder. Peter turned around to see Rob Garrett, the star running back of the football team and easily the most popular and athletic boy on campus. Rob had never been purposefully mean to Peter like so many of the kids at St. Thomas, but he hadn't noticed he was alive, either.

At least not until now.

"Hey, Hickman, I got a favor to ask." Rob kept his head low so the teacher wouldn't hear him talking. "Can I get your number so we can study once in a while?"

For a moment Peter thought Rob might be making some kind of joke. But almost as quickly he saw that the football star was serious. "Why me?"

"Because," Rob hissed, again trying to avoid being noticed by the teacher, "you're the smartest guy in school, and I need an A in this class."

"An A?" It hadn't occurred to Peter that jock kids like Rob might be interested in getting As. "What for?"

"Because I want a scholarship, okay?" Rob glanced at the teacher. "Will you help me or not?"

Peter agreed and slipped his phone number to Rob. That afternoon, Rob called and the two made plans to study three times a week at the school library. Peter wondered if Rob's friends would tease him if the two of them spent time together, but Rob never said a word.

Instead, as the weeks passed and they continued their study time, Peter began to think of Rob as a friend. Sometimes after they'd finished studying they'd talk for a few minutes. And every once in a while Maryanne Ellis would walk past and Peter would feel himself blushing.

"You like her, huh?" Rob would grin and cast a quick look at Maryanne as she walked past. "She's hot, Hickman. I don't know if you're her type."

Peter would push up the frames of his glasses and swallow hard. "Yeah...she's out of my league."

One day when they'd finished that same exchange, Rob studied him for a long moment. "Hey, Hickman. Can't you wear contact lenses instead of those..." Rob pointed at Peter's glasses. "Those bifocal things?"

Peter hesitated. "I guess. But contacts are a lot of work. These glasses came with the eye exam."

"I can tell." Rob raised an eyebrow. "Look, Hickman..." He lowered his head and leaned himself over the table so no one would hear his response. "Maybe if you let me help you, we can get somewhere with Maryanne."

"Really?" Peter was doubtful. The girl hung out with the most social kids on campus. If she actually knew Peter was alive, it was probably a bad thing.

Rob reached across the table and gave Peter a light punch in the shoulder. "Okay. Here's what we'll do."

The same way Peter had outlined American history notes, Rob laid out a plan that would make even the lamest social misfit into someone worth noticing. First he took Peter to the mall for a set of contacts and a haircut. Next they picked up a few new pairs of jeans and three sweaters—looser and roomier, from the teen section of the store, not the business attire his mother usually picked up in the men's department.

Finally, Rob taught Peter how to walk and stand with more confidence, relaxed and in control instead of hurried and nervous. Eye contact and a slower conversational style were the final touches. After three weeks of working together, Rob stood back and marveled.

"Peter, you look like a different guy."

Peter had to agree. Though nothing had changed

about his fascination with math or history, and though the school's social circles still were less important than figuring out where to apply for college, his look had changed. Rob couldn't wait to introduce him to Maryanne.

The winter dance was coming up, and Rob thought of another plan for Peter. A week later, when they were studying, he waited for Maryanne to pass by. This time, Rob called her over to the table and introduced Peter.

"Hi," Maryanne's smile was somewhat shy and surprised. "Are you new?"

Peter wasn't sure what to say. He looked at Rob and grinned. "Sort of."

After that, Rob flagged Maryanne down every day that week, and on Friday—as per the plan—Rob waited until Maryanne was sitting at their table and then he looked at his watch. "Shoot. I have a meeting with Coach West."

He was gone before either Peter or Maryanne could say anything.

In the resulting quiet, Peter smiled at Maryanne and raised one of his shoulders in a casual manner. "Hey, Maryanne...I've been meaning to ask you something."

She was comfortable around him now, seemingly unaware of his past social limitations, and accepted him as one of Rob's peers. She leaned her arms on the table and tilted her head to one side. "Okay, ask."

Peter could hardly believe what he was about to say, but he said it anyway. "Would you go to the winter dance with me?"

A giggle as soft as windchimes played on her lips, but without hesitation she nodded. "Sure, Peter. I'd love to."

Fourteen years later, Peter and Maryanne were happier than ever. But at least once a week he wondered about Rob Garrett. Wasn't there something he could do to thank the guy for setting him up with Maryanne? Where was he, anyway, and what was he doing? Had he found as much happiness in life as Peter had? Many times, Peter tried to find his old friend. Rob had attended Rutgers University, but the school was no help in shedding light on where Rob had gone after that.

Peter was working at his computer late one night when a thought hit him. The Internet had several sites where people could connect with old classmates. Inspired by the sudden possibility, Peter did a search and found an extensive listing of names and schools. He typed in the correct information, and in a matter of minutes he found Rob's name. The information listed was general, but it included his old friend's e-mail address. Peter jotted a quick note, asking if the recipient was indeed the Rob Garrett from St. Thomas High School and stating that he'd like to talk to him, if possible.

The next day, in his online mailbox, Peter found a response from the address. He opened the mail and found a letter from Rob's wife. Yes, Peter had reached the right person, but Rob was very busy. He rarely spent time on the computer. She included their phone number and address, located in Thousand Oaks, California.

At that last bit of information, Peter nearly jumped from his seat. "Maryanne!" he called out across the house and waited until she came down the hall and poked her head into his office.

"Yes?"

"How would you like to take a trip to California this weekend?"

Rob was just about at the end of his rope.

He and his wife and their oldest daughter, Tara,

had all been tested to see if their blood types matched Alicia's, but none of them did. Next the doctors checked the national donor bank, but that news was also bad. The chances of a match outside the family was one in ten thousand. The donor bank had nothing for their daughter, and Alicia's cancer was advancing at an alarming rate.

That day as they drove home from the doctor's office, Alicia fell asleep in the backseat of the car, and Rob and his wife prayed in whispered tones.

"We need a miracle, God. Find us a match for our little girl." Rob's voice cracked and he tightened his grip on the steering wheel. "Please."

When they pulled up in front of their house, a sedan was parked outside, and from what Rob could make out, a man was sitting in the driver's seat. "Who's that?" He narrowed his eyes and tried to make out the shape through his car's tinted windows.

His wife knit her eyebrows together. "No one I recognize."

As they parked their car and climbed out, the door of the sedan opened and a man stood up and waved at him. "Rob Garrett?"

Rob studied the man and found him vaguely

familiar, but from thirty yards away he couldn't place him. "Yes, how can I help you?"

"Rob, it's me! Peter Hickman!"

"Peter Hickman?" Rob's voice sounded tired, and his tone was only mildly surprised. Peter Hickman? The guy he'd befriended back at St. Thomas? The two hadn't spoken since graduation. "What are you doing in these parts?"

The man walked closer until finally Rob saw that he was indeed Peter Hickman. He was more filled out now and a smile stretched from one side of his face to the other. When he was closer, he reached out and shook Rob's hand. "I've wanted to find you for the past fourteen years, Rob. I can't believe I'm really here."

Rob wished he could appear more lively, more upbeat. But as his wife carried Alicia into the house, he felt like crying. How could he concentrate on this chance meeting with Peter Hickman when his little girl was dying?

Peter gushed on about how he and Maryanne had gotten married and how they had two children and how they couldn't be happier. "So you see," Peter slapped Rob on the back as the two headed for the house. "All these years I wanted to thank you. I kept wishing there was some way I could pay you back for what you did for me that year."

Rob brushed off the notion with a partial smile. "Don't worry about it, Peter." He took a seat in the living room and watched as Peter took the chair opposite him. "I'm glad it worked out so well."

Peter leaned back, his smile still full, eyes glowing. "How about you, Rob? How're things with you?"

At first, Rob didn't want to tell him. This was a chance meeting, after all, and the sooner Peter was gone, the sooner Rob could get back to worrying about Alicia. But in that moment, a Bible verse from a sermon earlier that week came to mind.

Where two or more are gathered, there I am also.

Rob made casual conversation as the Scripture played through his soul a few more times. Then finally, as though God himself were urging him to spill his heart, he froze midsentence. His hand came up to his face and he pinched the bridge of his nose with his thumb and forefinger.

"Rob? You okay?"

"No." The word was lost in a stifled sob. "Not really."

Peter slid to the edge of his chair and put his arm on Rob's shoulder. "What is it, buddy? Tell me."

And Rob told him everything.

When he was finished explaining about Alicia's dire situation, Peter stood and reached for his car keys. "I'm going to the hospital right now to have them draw blood. You never know, Rob. I could be a match. I'd hate to never find out."

The idea seemed almost ludicrous; no reason existed to believe Peter Hickman would be a blood match to his daughter. But it couldn't hurt. And Rob didn't have the energy to talk his old friend out of it.

Rob went with Peter to the hospital. Once his blood was drawn, Peter asked the nurse to reference his type to Alicia's case.

"I live out of town," he explained. "I'll need the results as soon as possible."

The nurse promised to phone the results in an hour, and Rob and Peter left the hospital. On the way home, they picked up a bucket of chicken, and they were just finishing dinner when the phone rang.

Telemarketers, Rob thought. He answered it on the third ring. "Hello?"

"Mr. Garrett?" The voice belonged to a woman, and it was brimming with excitement. "I have the results from Mr. Hickman's blood test."

"Yes?" Confusion welled up in Rob's chest. What was her enthusiasm about?

"He's a match, Mr. Garrett. A perfect match."

Rob fell in slow motion to his knees and hung his head. Peter Hickman was a perfect match for Alicia? How was it possible?

"What is it, Rob?" Peter was on his feet, standing behind him and touching the side of his arm. "What's the news?"

Rob wanted to talk but he couldn't. He was on holy ground, after all. Completely holy. Hours after he and his wife had prayed for a miracle, a man he hadn't seen in fourteen years walked up to him and a few hours later they had their daughter's match?

It was like something from a dream.

Rob stayed there, unmoving, trying to convince himself it was real. The phone fell to the floor, and he vaguely noticed his wife picking it up and learning the news for herself. In a matter of seconds, she relayed the information to Peter, and the three of them hugged and shouted and thanked God.

The surgery took place later that week, and no one was surprised when the transplant was a complete success. The miracle that had begun when Rob stepped into Peter's life and helped him meet Maryanne was finally complete. Peter had done the thing he'd always wanted to do—repay Rob for his kindness.

But only God could have brought the two together at that time, when Peter might repay his friend by giving away a part of himself and in the process saving Rob's little girl.

Angel in a Pickup

The two doctors had been friends and partners for twenty years. Their mannerisms and mindsets were so similar, they often joked that even their wives could barely tell them apart.

"Kindred spirits," William Sutter sometimes said.

And his best friend, Harry Bateman, would laugh and nod his head. "Kindred spirits."

Ten years after starting their practice, the two men found land in a remote canyon outside Cottonwood, Arizona. The drive was long and winding, and during monsoon season it could get treacherous, but the friends found the extra effort worth every minute.

They bought properties a few miles from each other and moved their families out into the desert.

One night in late August, Harry and his wife were watching a movie at a theater in Sedona when Harry was seized by a strange and sudden thought. Will was in trouble; he was sure of it.

About that time, a clap of thunder sounded above the movie and he jerked in his seat.

"It's just a storm, Harry." His wife took his hand, her voice barely a whisper. "Why so jumpy?"

"Will's in trouble. I have a feeling."

Both doctors had been Christians forever. Therefore, though their region was given to New Age philosophies, neither of them paid heed to the energies or feelings their patients sometimes talked about.

But this…this was something Harry simply couldn't deny. He grabbed hold of his seat's armrests and leaned close to his wife. "Let's go. I have to find him."

Twenty-one miles away, Will Sutter was in a world of trouble.

His wife and daughter were out of town visiting family on the east coast, so he'd gone out by himself for bread and milk. On the way home, just as he turned onto the canyon road that led to his house, a monsoon unlike any Will had ever seen before let loose.

Signs bordered the canyon warning of landslides

and flash floods, but in the ten years the families had lived off the road, neither had happened. Now, though, Will began to worry. Rain was coming down in sheets, and he couldn't be sure but it looked as if the earth along parts of the hillside had given way.

He moved slowly along, determined to make it home before the roads grew any worse. At that exact moment a car came from the opposite direction. As it neared, it halted and flashed its lights. Will stopped and rolled his window down just enough to see the driver, a white-haired man with light eyes that almost glowed in the dark of the stormy night.

"Can't get through," the man shouted at him. "Part of the road's gone."

Will had a sinking feeling in his gut. He had to get through; where would he spend the night if he didn't get home? Besides, the road couldn't be that bad. Whatever was wrong with it would be fixed the next morning, and everything would be fine.

As long as he managed to get home.

Will stuck his hand out the window and waved at the man. "Thanks," he yelled. "I'll take my chances."

The man looked hard at him and showed no signs of leaving. Will pulled himself from the man's stare and hit the gas pedal. *Strange guy,* he thought. And what was he doing on the remote canyon road, anyway? Will had never seen him before.

Will kept driving, going slower with each turn. After a few minutes, the strange man in the pickup truck was forgotten. Suddenly, without warning, a wall of water and mud crashed against his Suburban and pushed it toward the edge of the canyon. The drop was more than two hundred feet in that area and Will could do nothing to stop his vehicle from heading there.

"God! Help me!" Will shouted the words, glancing quickly at his surroundings. He had a few seconds at best before the flash flood and flowing hillside pushed him into the canyon. "Please, God...help!"

Then, suddenly, his Suburban jolted to a stop.

Will blinked, his fingers in a death grip around the steering wheel. What had happened? He looked out his driver-side window and saw that the water and mud were still flowing against his car, but not as strongly as before. Every few seconds he could feel his front tires slip a little toward the edge of the canyon, but still his vehicle held.

When it looked as if the flow had stopped, he tried to open his door and escape. But the movement of his body caused his Suburban to lurch a few feet closer to the edge. *Okay, God.* His heart pounded and he forced himself to stay as still as possible. *Give me a miracle, please. Get me out of this.*

Back at the theater, Harry and his wife had just climbed into their Explorer when a pickup truck pulled up next to the driver's door. Harry was trembling now, desperately worried about Will without any reason for feeling that way. He rolled down his window and looked at the man. Something about him seemed strange, otherworldly. His hair was bright white, and his eyes held an unnatural light.

Harry frowned at the man. "Can I help you?"

"Do you have a winch?" The man motioned back down the road. "There's a guy off Old Canyon Highway stuck in the mud. He's gonna need a winch."

Old Canyon Highway? That was the road he and Will lived on. Harry struggled to find his words. "I'm headed that way; I'll see what I can do."

The entire drive back toward Cottonwood, the feeling that Will was in danger only grew stronger for Harry. But as he turned onto the highway, he looked for a car stuck in the mud, since he'd promised the guy in the pickup he'd help.

"Do you think maybe this is a little crazy?" Harry's

wife took his hand and gave him a curious look. "Will is home tonight, remember? His family's out of town."

"I don't care." He met his wife's gaze and hoped she'd see how serious he was. "I've never felt like this in my life. He's in trouble, and God wants me to help him. That has to be it."

They kept driving, and Harry noticed sections of the road that were nearly buried in mud. The rain had stopped by then, but the damage it had caused was evident everywhere. "Flash floods," he told his wife. "That must be what that guy in the pickup was talking about."

One more turn and another straightaway and Harry's breath caught in his throat. There, ahead of them, was Will's car, the headlights flashing. It had slid sideways off the road toward the canyon's edge, and though a bank of mud remained wedged against the driver's door, a tree stump on the passenger side kept the Suburban from going over.

"Dear God, let me help him." Harry pulled over but stopped short of wading through the mud toward Will's car. "Will! It's me. Are you in there?"

"Yes!" Will's voice was higher than usual, tense and worried. "Stay there. I'm not stable. One wrong move and—"

At that instant, Will's car slid another few inches away from the stump, closer to the canyon's edge.

"I've got a winch. Hold on!" As Harry said the words, a chill ran down his spine. Suddenly he could picture the man in the pickup asking him if he had a winch, telling him that a man was stuck on Old Canyon Highway. How had the man driven from the remote canyon spot where Will was stuck to the theater parking lot in search of someone with a winch?

He had no time to analyze the situation. Cell phones didn't work on that stretch of the road, so a rescue would be up to him. If he left for help, it could be too late. Moving as fast as possible, he found his winch and, using a nearby tree for support, braced the Suburban in six places. Just as he attached the last rope, the Suburban pulled away from the tree stump and slid freely toward the edge of the canyon.

But Harry's ropes held, and the vehicle stopped a few feet short of going over.

"Praise God!" Will shouted from inside his car. "I'm getting out." He climbed through the back door, and using the ropes for support he made his way to Harry's car.

There the two men compared notes and realized something strange. They'd both had an encounter with the man in the pickup—a strange man with white hair and glowing eyes, whom neither of them had seen before that night.

"Do you think maybe…" Harry's wife was the first one to make the suggestion. "Could he have been an angel?"

The more the three talked about the possibility, the more it seemed the only answer. How else would Harry have felt driven to find his best friend at the very moment of his greatest need? And who else would have known where to find Harry at the theater, and in which direction to send him?

For a long moment no one said anything. They didn't have to, really. God in his miraculous wonder had said enough for all of them.

Back Together Again

Scott Miller was forever second-guessing himself as a single father. His wife had left him and their two children fifteen years ago, and now little Laura was a full-fledged teenager. For the most part, Scott figured he had a good relationship with Laura, but sometimes—nights like that one—he wasn't sure.

The evening had started out like any other, except it was Friday. For years, Fridays had been the nights Scott and Laura and her brother, Ben, settled down with a bag of microwave popcorn and watched a family movie. But three months earlier, when Laura turned sixteen, everything had begun to change. The occasional phone calls Laura once received became half a dozen every night.

Her friends seemed to have something fun going on every night, but Scott laid down the law early on.

"Only once a week, Laura. No more. You need family time and study time. You're too young to be out every few days."

Most of the time Laura agreed.

But that night she'd gotten a call from two of her favorite girlfriends. They were all planning to attend the same slumber party the next night, so they wanted to know if Laura could go shopping with them. Just for a few hours.

"Please, Dad? Come on, everyone's going."

Scott leaned against the living-room wall and leveled his gaze at his daughter. "You know the rule, Laura. Once a week."

"Yeah, but Dad, this isn't a night thing, it's shopping. Really. We'll be back before nine."

"Laura." He could feel the wall of his determination beginning to crumble. Times like this he wondered why he'd never remarried, why he'd never found someone to take away the loneliness he carried with him every day—someone who could be a mother for Laura. For a fraction of an instant he wondered about Becky Olsen, his first love. Becky would never have walked out on him, ever. If only he hadn't let her go after high school, she would be here now, offering Laura advice.

He sighed and searched his daughter's eyes. "Who's driving?"

"Susie's mother. She can pick me up and drop me off."

"Me, too?" Ben walked into the room and grinned at her. He was fifteen and loved giving Laura grief when it came to her friends.

"No," Scott dropped into the nearest chair and cocked his head at Ben. "Let's watch the game instead. Me and you." He looked at Laura. She'd be fine; this was Mill Creek, Washington, after all. The crime rate was one of the lowest in the nation. "Go ahead and go shopping."

Laura ran to him and threw her arms around his neck. "Thanks, Daddy. I promise I won't be long."

Becky Olsen normally worked the southern Oregon and California doctors' offices and medical centers. That was her territory as a sales manager for the largest pharmaceutical company in the nation. But earlier that week, one of her colleagues had begged a favor of her. Could she cover his territory and take Washington for the weekend?

Becky didn't hesitate. She was single and independent, and work hid the fact that she was lonely far too often. A lifetime ago, she'd been married with twin boys. But one spring night six years earlier, she'd arrived home from a business trip only to find that for the first time in her career, her family wasn't there to meet her.

Not until two hours later did she get the news.

They'd been coming to the airport when they were broadsided by a freight train at a dimly lit crossing near their home. All of them—her husband and boys—were killed instantly in the accident.

It took two years for Becky to get back to work, and when she did it was with a determination to remain single. She'd loved once, and lost. That was enough for an entire lifetime. The problem was her heart wasn't always in agreement. Some nights when she finished working her territory, she'd come home to her Portland, Oregon, apartment, pour herself a tall mug of coffee, sit at the kitchen table, and cry.

Not because she wanted another family. But because she wanted a friend. Her schedule kept her on the road far too often to develop any sort of consistent relationship, even with her neighbors. Once in a while, on those lonely nights, she found herself going back in time, back even farther than the family she'd loved. Back to her high-school days, when her closest friend had been her boyfriend, Scott Miller. They'd been kids, of course, but that hadn't stopped them from spending equal time laughing and playing and baring their hearts to each other.

Scott had gotten married years back, but still Becky wondered how he was doing. Not because she was interested in starting something up with him, but because he was an old friend. One of the best she'd had as a teenager.

Her thoughts cleared and she thought about the matter at hand. She needed to find her hotel, check in, and go over the notes for meetings she'd scheduled the next day at the nearby hospital. But first she needed to pick up a pair of nylons. It was almost eight o'clock when she pulled into a mall parking lot just north of Seattle.

Becky was about to take a parking spot when something caught her attention. She turned and saw a man in dark clothing walking behind a teenage girl. Becky could make out the girl's expression from where she sat in her car, and the look sent chills down her spine. The younger woman's eyes were wide and terror stricken.

Strange, Becky thought. Why was he walking

behind her? If the man was her father, why weren't they walking side by side or at least with her farther in front of him instead of so close? The way it looked now, the girl was almost being pushed toward a car at the back of the parking lot.

Becky drove down the row and turned up the next so she was facing the pair. She watched them reach a beat-up sedan, one that looked out of place in that high-end area of Seattle.

God . . . What's going on? Is the girl in trouble?

Follow them, daughter. Follow.

The answer was more of a perception than an actual audible voice, but it resonated in Becky's heart the same as if God had shouted the words at her with a bullhorn. Moving at a slow, steady rate so the man wouldn't notice her, Becky eased her car closer. When the man and the girl pulled away in the car, she stayed behind at a distance that didn't seem to catch his attention.

Becky's heart began to race as they turned onto the main road and started south. What was she doing? If God wanted her to follow the car, then the girl must be in trouble somehow. But she'd seen nothing that proved the man meant the girl harm.

She pulled her cell phone from her purse and

flipped it open. If she called for help, the police would want a reason, an indication that this was more than merely an intense intuition.

The man turned onto a lesser traveled street, and finally Becky knew she had no other option. If he led them into a deserted area, he'd certainly see her following him, and then the girl could be in more trouble than before. For that matter, if he had a gun, she and the girl could both be at risk.

Without giving the matter another thought, Becky dialed 9-1-1 and waited.

A voice came on the line in an instant. "Nine-one-one. What's your emergency?"

"I'm following a man whom I believe has kidnapped a teenage girl." Becky ran her tongue over her lips and tried to sound believable. "She looked scared to death."

The emergency operator asked for Becky's location and she gave it. Three minutes later, a police car with flashing lights came up behind Becky, passed her, and pulled over the man and the teenage girl.

Becky stopped also and sat in the car while the drama played out. One officer asked the man at the wheel to step out while his partner patted him down. That's when Becky saw it.

The second officer froze and then pulled a gun from the man's pocket. For an instant, the man tried to run away, but the first officer tackled him to the ground, and within seconds the man was cuffed and placed in the back of the squad car.

Becky climbed out of her car then, her knees trembling from what she'd just witnessed. She approached the car, where officers were talking to the girl, and explained that she was the witness, the person who had seen the man lead the girl through the parking lot.

The teenager was sobbing, shaking from fear and explaining what had happened. "We...we were shopping and I forgot my wallet in the car. So...I went out to get it and I felt—" She pointed to her side. "—something against my waist." She sobbed twice and squeezed her eyes shut. "I looked and that...that man had a gun pointed at me. He told me to start walking or he'd shoot."

Becky felt the color drain from her face. What if she hadn't heeded the thought from God, the direction to follow the car? The girl would be on her way to being raped and possibly killed. The police were making their report, so Becky approached the girl, introduced herself, and explained how she had witnessed the man forcing her to the car and called for help.

Though she was still terrified, still shaking, the girl got out of the car and shook Becky's hand. "Thank you so much." She folded her arms and began to shiver. "Could...could you wait for my dad to get here? He's on his way; he'd want to thank you, too."

Becky agreed. Not so much so the girl's father could thank her, but because the girl looked like she needed someone besides the police to stay with her. Five minutes passed, and finally a Jeep pulled up behind Becky's car. It was dark, but Becky watched as a tall man jumped out and ran toward them. His eyes were locked only on the teenage girl.

"Laura...thank God." He took the girl in his arms and held her.

Becky moved back a few steps, intent on bidding the father and daughter a quiet good-bye and getting on her way. But the girl pulled from her father's arms. "You have to meet Becky. She's the one who followed us and called for help."

The man turned to Becky, and suddenly they both

froze. Becky stared at his face, his eyes, and gasped quietly. "Scott?"

"Becky...How did you..."

"I'm here on business. I..." Becky's legs trembled, and her heart beat in a pattern she didn't recognize. "I can't believe this."

Laura was still standing next to her father, and now she looked from Becky to her dad and back again. "You know each other?"

"Yes. In fact, we do." Scott smiled and gave Becky a hug, one that stirred up memories for both of them.

In a matter of minutes, with traffic whizzing by and police officers finishing up their report, Scott and Becky learned that each was single, and that in fact they'd been wondering about each other for years. When they left that night, they went to a diner and caught up. Not until the evening was almost finished did Laura put what had happened into context.

"We were part of a miracle tonight," she said as she sipped on a glass of root beer. "God brought you two friends together, and he did it by having Becky save my life. Only God does that sort of stuff."

Scott and Becky agreed Laura was right. And

they still remind themselves often of that miracle, especially each June when they celebrate their wedding anniversary. And remember the strange and miraculous way God brought them back together again.

In Need of a Friend

Bonner Davis knew the end was near, but he could do nothing to change his situation. He had advancing throat cancer, mounting medical bills, and no way to pay for the experimental treatment that could save his life.

A retired forest ranger, Bonner and his wife, Angela, lived in North Carolina where they existed on his meager pension and a faith bigger than the Smoky Mountains. Once in a while, Bonner would share his fears with Angela. She was his best friend, and though he looked forward to heaven, he didn't want to leave her.

Angela's answer was always the same. "God knows what we need, Bonner. I'm praying for a miracle, and somehow...somehow I believe he'll give us one."

*   *   *

In nearby Spartanburg, millionaire Olsen Matthews was celebrating his sixtieth birthday. Single and without any close friends, Olsen chose to spend his day in the air. He was a novice pilot who always felt more complete when he was alone in his small Cessna plane.

Sunshine reigned that afternoon, and Olsen savored the familiar rush as he took to the air. He'd been in the air twenty minutes when the rush faded to a sort of soul-searching, which often happened when Olsen flew. What was life about, anyway? He had more money than he knew what to do with, but not a single person he could call a friend.

Sure, Olsen had advisors and peers he did business with. But he had no family, no friend who cared about him.

This time as he flew, gazing down at the rolling hills and valleys, another thought filled Olsen's heart: *What about God?* All his life he'd denied the idea of both creation and Creator, but now…with his life waning toward the sunset years, he sometimes wondered.

What if God was real? What if he had a few things to do before he died in order to be right with that

God? The possibility set his nerves on edge and made him wish once more for a friend. Someone he could share his thoughts with. Perhaps even someone who knew something about God and why so many people believed in him.

Olsen was about to turn his plane around and soar back over the mountains when he heard a sharp pop. At the same instant, the engine cut out. Olsen felt a wave of adrenaline rush through his veins, but he stayed calm. He'd never lost an engine before, but there were ways to handle the situation. He flipped a series of switches designed to restart the motor, but none of them worked.

Okay, he told himself, *time for Plan B.*

If the engine wouldn't reengage, Olsen's only hope was to glide the plane in lazy circles toward the ground and make an emergency landing. By using the wing flaps and other instruments, he could slow the speed of the aircraft and still walk away.

At the same time, the plane could catch a wrong current and plummet to the ground.

"God!" He called the name out loud, and he heard the fear in his voice. "If you're real, help me. I'm not ready to go."

Two minutes passed in textbook fashion, but

then, as Olsen had feared, a strong current dropped the right wing of the plane and the craft began to tumble. Olsen had another thousand feet to go before hitting land, but as the plane fell he spotted a lake. *Water,* he thought. *That's my only hope.* Landing in the trees or on the hilly ground would cause the Cessna to disintegrate on impact.

"Water, God...If you're listening, lead me to the water."

The ground was rushing up to meet him. Suddenly his plane fell to the left and Olsen could see he was going to hit the small lake. The last thing he remembered was the sound of water breaking over his plane and the rush of ice-cold wetness filling the cabin. Suddenly the craft jolted to a stop and Olsen smacked his head on the doorframe.

After that, there was only darkness.

Bonner was pouring himself a glass of iced tea when he saw a small plane tumble into view and freefall into the lake at the edge of his property.

"Angela, quick! Call 9-1-1. A plane just crashed into the lake."

After years of outdoor training and living, Bonner had always been in good shape. But the cancer medication had taken its toll, and as he ran toward the lake he could barely catch his breath. Fifty yards, a hundred, two hundred, and finally he reached the shore.

The situation was more grim than he'd thought.

The wing of the plane jutted out of the water, but it was otherwise buried in a section of the lake some ten feet deep and seventy-five yards off shore. No one else must have seen the crash, because he was the only one standing at the water's edge looking for signs of life.

His heart raced within him, and he still hadn't caught his breath. But he had no choice. Whoever was in the plane was drowning even at that very moment. Before he jumped in, he uttered a silent prayer. *God, if I don't make it back to shore, let Angela know how much I love her.*

Then he dove in and headed as hard and fast as he could toward the plane. Because of his weakened condition, the swim took Bonner twice as long as it normally would have. After five minutes, he reached the wing and though his lungs were already burning from the effort, he sucked in as much air as he could and dove down. His heart pounded, filling his senses with an urgency that drove him deep, deeper toward the fuselage door. He tried twice to open it, and finally on the third try, the door swung free.

Bonner was out of air.

He swam to the surface, nauseated from the effort, grabbed another breath, and went back down. This time he found the pilot in seconds and felt around until he was sure the person was alone. Feeling as though he could die at any moment, Bonner dragged the unconscious man to the surface. They weren't out of danger yet, and that terrified Bonner because, simply, he was out of energy.

Help me, God. Help me. Bonner let the words play in his mind again and again as he kept himself and the man afloat. It took no time to realize that the pilot wasn't breathing.

Swimming with a strength that wasn't his own, Bonner dragged the pilot back to shore. On the beach, despite his exhaustion he managed to administer CPR. He was three minutes into the process when an emergency crew arrived and took over. He barely made it to the edge of a grove of trees before he dropped to the ground, unable to go on.

At almost the same time, Angela came running toward him. "Bonner!" She waved down one of the paramedics and Bonner heard her explain about his cancer. "Help him, please."

The emergency worker moved quickly and hooked Bonner up to intravenous fluids. They took him to the local hospital, and four hours later he was ready to go home. Before he left, he heard the news about the pilot. The CPR had saved his life.

Bonner figured that might be the end of the situation, but the next day he received a visit from the pilot.

"My name's Olsen Matthews. You saved my life." The man shook Bonner's hand. "The paramedics said you were praying out loud, thanking God at the scene."

"Yes." Bonner stared at the man. He looked wonderful, considering he should have died in the plane crash. "My wife and I were both praying."

The man's eyes grew watery. "Thank you for that." He motioned toward Bonner's house. "Could I come in?"

The two talked for almost an hour. Olsen explained that he'd heard from his doctors about Bonner's cancer. "I have a check for you, something to help with your medical costs." The man shrugged and gave Bonner a slight smile. "Maybe it'll help you get the care you need."

Then Olsen asked Bonner about God. And with Angela at his side, Bonner told him about their faith and about living a life right before God. At the end of the conversation, Olsen and Bonner prayed.

"Could you be my friend, Bonner? Someone I could visit now and then, someone to talk to about God?"

A smile lifted the corners of Bonner's mouth. He squeezed Angela's hand. "Definitely."

"Good." Olsen stood to leave. "I was asking God about a friend when I crashed. And now he's worked everything out." Olsen walked to the door, looked over his shoulder, and grinned. "I think he's going to work everything out for you, too, Bonner."

When the man was gone, Bonner turned to Angela and remembered the check. "He gave me something, a thank-you gift."

"Well, open it up." Angela stood beside him, peering at the folded check.

Bonner did, and both he and Angela fell silent, shocked.

The check was for one million dollars. In the note section it read only, "Use this to get better."

Bonner did just that. In the months that followed he tried the costly experimental treatment. Three years later, in one of their many times together, Bonner and Olsen agreed that God had done more than take part in the miracle of Olsen's rescue and Bonner's healing.

He also gave them the miracle of new friendship.

In the Nick of Time

As Taylor Evans climbed the damaged utility pole that cloudy afternoon in Oklahoma City, two thoughts occurred to him. First, he hadn't heard from his best friend, Aaron, in six months. And second, he no longer expected to.

Taylor stared at the light fixture some thirty feet above him and began to climb. He hadn't pictured himself working for the electric company when he graduated from college, but the job had come up, and now he was close to being made foreman. The job paid well, tasks were usually simple to complete, and after twenty years he'd have a better pension than most.

That afternoon, the problem was with the light itself. The bulb had been changed the week before, but now the new one had burned out. No doubt the wires were frayed, and it was Taylor's job to determine where.

He glanced at the increasing clouds overhead and whispered a familiar prayer. *Get me down safely, God. Get me down safely.*

His climb continued five feet, ten, closer to the light fixture. As he moved, his mind wandered again and images of Aaron came once more. They'd been closer than brothers, able to read each other's thoughts almost before they had time to think them. High school had been a blast, the two of them playing football and basketball for Central High School, and the same had been true for junior college.

Back then, Aaron had been good enough to win a scholarship, if only he would have worked harder on his academics. His grade-point average was such that he talked Taylor into spending their first two years at the local community college, where they could both play football and Aaron could hope for a scholarship once his grades were up.

The first season was going better than either of them had dreamed when the injury happened.

Aaron was a tight end. One night a particular play had him cutting left and running ten yards for the catch. But a linebacker from the opposing team caught his pattern almost as soon as the ball was snapped. Aaron took a direct, full-force blow to his knee and collapsed to the ground. He had to be taken from the field on a stretcher to the hospital, where doctors delivered the devastating news.

His knee was destroyed. Several operations would be necessary to give Aaron back mobility and range, and he would have to learn to walk again. But his days of playing football were over forever.

That was the beginning of the end, Taylor thought, as he kept climbing the utility pole. He'd prayed for Aaron for months and years on end after that, rescuing him from parties where he was stone drunk, taking him to counseling centers where he could get help for the depression that plagued him, and most of all telling him about God.

But Aaron didn't want help, didn't want to hear about answers.

Instead he drew farther from Taylor every year. Finally, that past spring, Aaron told Taylor their friendship was over.

"I don't want your answers, Taylor." Aaron's voice was cold and bitter, without a trace of the warm humor that had been his trademark through high school. "Leave me alone, Taylor. We're finished."

Three times since then Taylor had called. But always Aaron's attitude was the same. And now... now that fall was here, Taylor was beginning to accept the idea. The guy he'd thought he'd stay friends with forever was finally and completely out of his life.

Aaron Grant walked out of the church hall and smiled at the stormy sky above. How had he been so blind before, and how could he have let losing football nearly cost him his soul?

Two months earlier, Aaron had been at a bar, too drunk to sit up straight, when his former coach walked in and spotted him. The man came up alongside Aaron, his face a mix of sorrow and surprise. "Aaron, how are you?"

Aaron didn't remember much about the conversation, only that his words were too slurred to understand. After a few more attempts, his old coach had shrugged and walked away.

Even in his drunken stupor, Aaron realized what had just happened. The man he'd played ball for, the man who'd dreamed with him and believed in him, had just walked away from him in disgust.

Suddenly every poor decision he'd made since his

knee injury came flooding back, and there on the stool where he could barely manage to sit, Aaron hit rock bottom. The next day he was seized with remorse for the way he'd treated his best friend. Hadn't Taylor always been there? Hadn't he only wanted the best for Aaron?

Memories flooded his heart all that morning, times when Taylor had forced him through his rehabilitation exercises, times when the two of them had run together, with Taylor always shouting at him to push harder, faster.

Now that he'd made a decision to change, Aaron wanted to call Taylor more than anything, but he knew he couldn't.

Not yet.

First he would get his act together, find out about this God that Taylor talked about so often, and walk away from alcohol altogether. Then, in a few months, he'd be ready. He could call Taylor and thank him for being the best friend anyone could ever have. And maybe, if God was willing, there would be some small way he could thank Taylor for never giving up. Even when Aaron asked him to do so.

The next two months passed in a blur of intensity. The same effort Aaron had once given on the football field he now gave to getting his life together. He sought counseling for his depression and alcohol abuse and took a job working at the local supermarket. At night he started his college classes up again, and three times a week he attended a church near his house for services and Bible studies.

That afternoon, with storm clouds building overhead, Aaron knew it was time. He'd known it from the moment they read the Bible verse for the day, the one that talked about encouraging each other daily. Encouragement had been Taylor's ultimate gift to Aaron, even though that gift had been rejected. Now, though, Aaron could hardly wait to get home and call Taylor.

It was time he and Taylor reconnected, time for Aaron to start repaying the favor and do some encouraging of his own. As he drove across town, rain began to fall and in the distance sharp bolts of lightning pierced the afternoon sky.

Aaron smiled and hummed a song about God's grace. No storm could dim his excitement. He was ten minutes from home, ten minutes from calling Taylor and making everything right again. No matter what else the day might bring, Aaron could hardly wait.

*   *   *

The storm was making Taylor nervous. Clouds shooting off lightning bolts were drawing nearer every few minutes.

Taylor was at the top of the utility pole now, and he knew the protocol: Get down immediately in case of an electrical storm. But Taylor had worked the job for long enough to know how much time he had. Ten minutes at least, maybe fifteen. He was nervous, sure, but he wouldn't be stupid.

He opened the glass fixture and saw the problem—frayed wires at the back of the bulb, so damaged that one of them wasn't connected at all. Taylor went right to work, all the while keeping one eye on the storm. *Three minutes, God. Help me be safe for three minutes. Then I'll be done and I'll climb back down.*

At that instant his cell phone rang.

Because he was a specialist for the company, his personal phone had two distinct rings. One for normal incoming calls and one with short staccato beeps for emergencies. This time the ring was short staccato beeps. Taylor let his head fall forward in frustration. An emergency? Now? When he was so close to completing the task and getting down the pole?

For a single moment, he thought about ignoring

the call, but that would never do. Someone could be trapped on a pole or injured on a job site. When the ring came in as an emergency, he had to take it. He flipped his phone from his pocket, holding onto the pole and his safety harness, and barked a short hello.

A few words sounded on the other end, but nothing Taylor could make out. His frustration doubled. This happened once in a while when the utility pole would interfere with phone reception.

"Fine." He mumbled the word and began the arduous climb back down the pole. When he reached the bottom, rain began to fall, and he slipped inside his car to make the call. At that exact moment, Taylor felt the hair on the back of his neck stand straight up. Before he could blink, a blinding bolt of lightning zapped the utility pole twenty feet away, slicing across the very spot where Taylor had been working a minute earlier.

The place where he'd still be if it weren't for the phone call.

Seconds passed, and Taylor could do nothing but stare at the smoking tip of the utility pole. He would have been dead instantly from the jolt, no question about it. Finally, as the shock began to wear off, Taylor drew a steadying breath and closed his eyes. *God, you saved me from certain death. Thank you . . . and thank you for whoever called me on the—*

His thoughts came to an abrupt stop. He hadn't checked on the message. Somewhere someone was having an emergency, and they had been counting on him to answer his phone. He pressed a series of buttons to check the previous caller's phone number and saw it was both familiar and local. But he couldn't place where he'd seen it before.

He pressed the Send button and waited.

On the third ring, Aaron Grant answered. "Hello?"

"Aaron?" Taylor's mind was reeling. Of course. The number was Aaron's landline, a number Taylor had rarely called since Aaron took most of his messages through his cell phone.

"Taylor, you won't believe it." The man sounded serious, more clear headed than he had in years. "I've changed, Taylor. I had to call you and tell you so myself. Can we meet for dinner sometime this week?"

Could they meet for dinner? Taylor gave a light shake of his head and tried to clear the cobwebs. Something wasn't making sense here. "Did you call me on my emergency line?"

A pause filled the other end. "No. Just your normal cell phone number."

"That's impossible." Taylor glanced out the window at the black mark near the top of the utility pole. "I was working. I wouldn't have come down if..."

Suddenly the pieces fell into place.

The ring had come through as an emergency by some divine mistake, some God-directed miracle. A chuckle sounded in his throat and he realized his palms were sweaty. How appropriate that God would use Aaron this way, just when it seemed that the two might never talk again. "You know something, Aaron?" His words were careful and filled with sincerity as he spoke to his long-lost friend. "I think you just saved my life."

"No man, that's not it." Aaron's voice was troubled. "I'm calling to thank you for saving mine. Hoping you'll... hoping you'll forgive me."

"Tell you what." Taylor slipped his keys into the ignition. "Let's meet at the diner near the junior college. You aren't going to believe what just happened."

Miracle of Love

Sarah Johnson had one prayer for her son, Robbie: That one day soon he would find a friend. Sarah and her husband, Karl, had recently moved from Rhode Island to the Pacific Northwest, a transfer necessary for his work as a computer systems analyst.

But in the process, Robbie lost every friend he'd ever had.

Robbie wasn't like other boys. He couldn't run or talk or think like the rest of them because Robbie had Down syndrome. Back in Rhode Island, he'd attended a regular public grade school where he took instruction in a special-education classroom. At that school, the other students were familiar with him, and as a group they'd taken a liking to him. He was invited to birthday parties, and at school functions he was always surrounded by other children.

"I have lots of friends," Robbie would tell Sarah. "Friends are God's way of telling you he loves you."

"Yes," Sarah would agree. "God definitely loves you, Robbie."

Robbie would beam and all would be right with the world.

But ever since the move, Robbie had been quiet and sullen. After school, Sarah or Karl would ask him about his day, and he'd stare at the ground, lost in thought for a moment. Then he'd look up and say, "It was bad. No friends."

They'd lived in their new location for three months, and they were four weeks into the school year, when Sarah and Karl had a meeting with Robbie's teacher.

"I'd like to find out more about Robbie." The teacher had a stack of Robbie's papers on the desk, but she kept her hands folded on top of them. "He seems very lonely, but he isn't trying to connect with the kids in class."

Sarah and Karl were quiet for a moment. Finally Karl spoke up. "I think he's missing his friends back in Rhode Island." Karl managed a smile. "He was quite popular back there."

The teacher nodded, a look of empathy on her

face. "Then perhaps it's time to get Robbie involved in something extracurricular. Music lessons, maybe. Or a drawing class. Children with Down syndrome typically enjoy exploring their artistic side."

Sarah tried to picture Robbie finding interest in piano or drawing. Robbie was an active child, one who but for a single chromosome would've been the fastest runner in class, the one most likely to star on the football field one day. Sports ran innately through him, but so far life had offered him no way to express that desire.

"Robbie's an active boy." Karl spoke for both of them. "Art classes are fine, but he needs to connect with kids on a physical level."

The teacher gave another thoughtful nod and promised to look for such opportunities. "In the meantime, let's keep hoping he'll open up with his classmates. That would give him a wonderful support structure."

That night, Robbie came home from school and found Sarah in the living room. "I wanna run track. Please, can I, Mom?"

Sarah's heart sank. Robbie couldn't possibly run with the school's track team. Even if they were only fifth graders and not very fast, Robbie wouldn't have a chance at keeping up. Even more, the school would most likely not let him. She reached her hand out for Robbie's and bit her lip. *God, give me the words here.* When her voice felt steady enough to speak, she narrowed her eyes at Robbie. "Son, I'm not sure that track is the best thing for you."

"But I could make friends running." He turned and took four hurried, cloddish steps. "See, Mom. I can run. Really, I can."

Sarah sighed. "We'll see, Robbie. I'll talk to your dad tonight."

After Robbie was in bed, Sarah told Karl about their son's intentions. "He wants to be on the school team, Karl. We can't have that; he'll be the laughingstock of the school. Not only that, the other runners at the meet will have a problem running against someone with a disability."

Karl anchored his elbow on top of the table and rested his head against his open hand. "I don't know; might be worth looking into." He shrugged. "Could be good for him."

Sarah didn't see how. The boy needed friends, not critics. A group of track-star kids wasn't bound to have any need for someone slow and lumbering like Robbie. Still, the next morning Sarah called the office to check out the track program, and she learned that Robbie would be welcome.

"We would place him in his own category, for disabled kids," the school secretary explained. "Unless other kids with similar disabilities join track, he'd take first place every time."

First place every time? Running races by himself? Sarah wasn't sure Robbie would appreciate that, but at least he'd be on the team. She talked it over with Robbie and Karl that night.

"You might be the only special boy on the team." Karl tried to convey the picture to Robbie. "Would you care if you're the only one running your race?"

Robbie angled his head and looked at the ceiling, as if the decision required extra thought. He shifted his gaze back to Karl. "Would I be on the team?"

"Yes." Karl gave him a crooked smile. "You'd be on the team."

"Okay, then." Robbie raised up his hand and flashed a victory sign. "Let's do it."

The first week of practice was Robbie's best at the new school. Every day he came home a bit more excited about the chance to run in a race, the opportunity to be part of a team. Sarah and Karl wanted to watch practice, to see how the other kids were accepting Robbie, but they resisted. He would have to survive without their support if he was going to survive at all.

Track season opened with its first meet the following Friday. Sarah and Karl took seats in the stands and waited for Robbie's race. His coach had explained that his event would be among the first set, so he wouldn't have too long to wait before feeling like he was part of the action.

Still, Sarah was nervous. She found her son in a crowd of kids stretching with one of the coaches and tried to determine if the other athletes were including him. After a few minutes she saw one of the girls slide closer to him. Robbie had been stretching over the wrong leg, and she corrected him.

"Karl, watch." Sarah pointed at the scene, her voice a whisper.

"I see it." He grinned.

At that moment, Robbie nodded and flashed the girl a smile that was visible across the field. Sarah felt her heart soar. It was working; Robbie really was making friends on the team. Still, it would be impossible to tell if the track team was a good place for Robbie until after his race.

Twenty minutes later, the announcer called for

runners to report for the Special-100. Again, a nervous fluttering rose up in Sarah's stomach. *Please, God. Let him feel good about this. Help him look past the fact that he's the only one in the race.*

"What's that?" Karl leaned closer and pointed to the starting line. A race was getting ready to start, and Robbie's event would be immediately afterward. He was stretching some fifteen yards beyond the starting line, the way he should. But four other runners were stretching, too.

"Strange." Sarah squinted at the students and saw they were in conversation with Robbie. The race in progress finished up, and Sarah watched Robbie take his place at the starting line.

On either side of him, the four other runners lined up, too.

"I thought..." Karl's statement hung in the air.

The starting gun sounded, and the runners were off. Robbie led the way, pumping and plodding down the track, face down at times for all his intensity. And behind him, never closer than a few yards, the other runners jogged along, their faces serious, but relaxed, as if this was a run they had worked all week for.

Watching Robbie run a hundred yards would've

been painful if it weren't for the other runners. Instead, Sarah felt as if she were caught up in a dream. Robbie was running a race with other able-bodied children—and winning. He crossed the finish line with both arms raised, and instantly the trailing runners enveloped him in a group hug. One of them took Robbie's hand and pumped it in the air in a victory dance.

Sarah put her fingers over her mouth and blinked back tears. What had happened out there? She looked at Karl and saw him clench his jaw. He cleared his throat and his chin quivered some. "That…" He waited until he had more control. "That was amazing."

A few minutes later, Robbie was still on the field when one of the other boys who had run with him wandered up into the stands. Sarah couldn't resist, so she waved him over.

"Hi." She nodded at the boy. "I'm Robbie's mother."

The boy stopped and smiled. "Hi."

"So…" Sarah searched for the words. "How come you and those other kids ran with Robbie?"

"Oh, that." A knowing look flashed in the boy's eyes. "Coach told us we were all special. The kids who worked hardest got to run with Robbie."

Sarah's throat grew thick as she let the boy's words sink into her heart. She reached for Karl's hand and squeezed it, her sign to him that she couldn't speak.

Karl slid closer to the edge of the bench. "Did the coach tell you to let Robbie win?"

"No. Not at all." The boy looked serious, as though the answer was obvious. "We were pacing him." He paused. "You know, cheering him on."

"Oh." Karl was silent for a moment, his grip tightening on Sarah's hand. "Thanks. I'm sure...I'm sure that meant a lot to Robbie."

The season continued, and each week the same thing happened. The coach would select the four best performers from the week and allow them the privilege of running in the special race with Robbie. Always they stayed a few feet behind him, pacing him, cheering him on. And always Robbie took first place, fist raised in the air, a victory smile spread across his face.

Sarah asked Robbie often about running track, and whether he was enjoying being a part of the team. Robbie's answer was always an emphatic yes. "I have friends, Mom. A whole team of friends."

Finally it was the last meet of the season. Fifteen minutes after the start, the coach found Sarah and Karl in the stands. The man had been so kind, such an answer to their prayers that Robbie have a friend, and several times through the season they'd thanked him.

Now he ran up to them, his eyes wide. "We want Robbie to run in the 400 relay; is that okay with you?"

Sarah blinked, confused. "The four-hundred? You mean for special kids?"

"No." The coach grinned, and his eyes grew soft. "The four-hundred relay. The last event in the race."

"But, coach..." Karl bit his lip. "Your team hasn't lost that event all year."

"Exactly." The coach looked from Sarah and Karl back to the field where Robbie was waiting, probably for the thumbs-up. The coach glanced at them again. "The other school forfeited that event. We need to run it for the points, but it's an automatic win." He smiled. "As long as we complete the race, we take an automatic first in the event and go to districts."

Sarah and Karl gave their blessing, and two hours later, after Robbie had completed his special run, he lined up with the other athletes for the 400.

"Looks like he's got the first leg," Karl whispered to her.

Before the race started, Sarah prayed. *God, this is*

as close as Robbie will ever get to fitting in with able-bodied kids. Please . . . let it be a good experience.

The gun sounded and Robbie was off, his feet pumping harder than before. In his hand was the baton and with each stride he stretched out. From the other three spots around the track, his teammates cupped their hands around their mouths and cheered hard for him. Then, fifty yards into his section of the relay, Robbie tripped and flew forward, hands outstretched. He skidded along the rough track surface and then settled to a stop, motionless.

Sarah was on her feet, stifling a gasp. Her fingers covered her mouth, and in a quiet whisper she leaned close to Karl. "Is he okay?"

Karl only shook his head and leaned forward. "Finish the race, Robbie. Come on. The team needs a finish here."

That's when they noticed something happening. From the three spots along the track where the other three runners were waiting, each of them began running toward Robbie. Together they helped him to his feet, and one of them found the baton in the grass where it had fallen. Only then did Sarah see Robbie's injuries. His knees and upper legs were badly scraped and bleeding; the same with his hands and arms.

"Karl!" She started to stand up. "He can't keep going."

Karl held his hand out in front of her, forcing her to stay seated. "Wait. It's okay, Sarah. Let's see what's going to happen."

When it was obvious to his teammates that Robbie couldn't keep running, two of the boys made a chair with their arms, and together, carrying Robbie, all four runners trudged to the next station. When they reached it, Robbie handed his baton to one of the boys carrying him.

At that point, the fans began rising to their feet, cheering and clapping on the team as they trudged on, all three able-bodied runners shoulder to shoulder, Robbie carried in the middle.

A hundred yards later the baton was handed to the next boy helping to carry Robbie. And just before the last hundred yards, that boy handed the baton to their fourth teammate.

When they crossed the finish line, all four runners raised their hands and then formed a group hug, jumping and pumping their fists in the air.

Sarah and Karl watched them from their place in the stands, surrounded by people who understood exactly what they'd just seen. The runners on the field were more than winners. They were a team, and more than that, they were friends.

Sarah and Karl had prayed for the miracle of acceptance for their son. That prayer was answered a hundred-fold.

A Friend in Need

The church meeting was set to begin in ten minutes, and still Adam Murphy couldn't believe he was there. He had promised himself he'd never be back, never step foot in a church again. Yet here he was, not by force, but because of the love of one very special friend.

And all because of an event so amazing and unbelievable, it could be nothing but a miracle.

The pianist played something slow and meaningful in the distance, and Adam glanced over his shoulder as someone entered the sanctuary. It was him—the man who had shown friendship when Adam deserved nothing but judgment and disdain. That man was Will Fredericks. Now Will shuffled in through the back door, spotted him, and smiled. In his slow and painful way, Will made the walk to the place where Adam was sitting.

"You came." Adam slid over and patted the place beside him.

"Wouldn't have missed it." Will sat down and gave Adam a hug. "I feel like God's got another miracle up his sleeve."

Adam wasn't sure what Will meant by that, and he didn't ask. Instead he stared at the roughly hewn cross up on the stage. And slowly, gradually, the yesterdays began to fall away until he was back there again, the summer of his twenty-fifth year.

The year his life changed forever.

Back then, Adam had felt like the happiest man in the world. After a rough childhood and teenage years fraught with drug abuse and petty theft, at age twenty-two Adam moved across the country to Portland, Oregon, and took an apartment in a low-rent district. Two days later he met Will Fredericks.

Will was in his late seventies, a retired police officer still in love with his wife of fifty-five years. Will and Wanda took a liking to Adam from the beginning, asking him to church service and inviting him to their home for Sunday dinners. Adam had no trouble accepting the dinner offer, but going to church was another thing.

"God wouldn't know what to do with a guy like

me." The corners of Adam's mouth would lift in a half-hearted grin. "He's a lot more comfortable with people like you and Wanda."

Still, Will continued to ask. Three months after his move to Portland, Adam took fresh stock of his life and realized how far he'd come. He had a job, he was free of drugs, and he had a best friend—Will Fredericks. The two would meet in the afternoon, when Adam was finished with his job at a local auto shop. Sometimes they'd talk about current events, other days they would play checkers or share some of Wanda's famous lemonade.

Summer was coming, and Will suggested Adam attend a downtown festival on the waterfront. A nationally known evangelist was speaking that day, and Adam felt drawn to the message.

"No matter who you are . . . no matter where you've been or what you've done, God isn't surprised. He already knows." The man smiled, and something about the sparkle in his eyes reminded Adam of his friend, Will. "Here's the best part—God loves you anyway. He loves you and he's waiting even now for you to turn around and come to him."

Adam moved closer and closer to the front of the crowd, caught up in the message. When it was over, he realized he'd been standing next to a blonde, blue-eyed young woman about his age. Adam smiled at her. "Great stuff, huh?"

"Yeah." She shrugged, shy. "I can't wait to hear what he says tonight."

"Tonight?"

"Sure." The girl giggled. "He's here all weekend."

Adam glanced back at the small crowd of people gathered around the speaker. "I guess I didn't know."

"I heard him last year. He's great every time he talks."

The brief conversation was about to end; Adam could sense it. He hesitated, but only for the blink of an eye. Then he stuck his hand out. "I'm Adam Murphy."

"Hi." Another shy smile. "I'm Brenda Gellen."

Adam motioned toward the water. "Wanna take a walk?"

"Sure."

They talked for an hour near the river's edge. Adam told her about his past and how he'd cleaned up his life.

"But sometimes I still feel empty."

Brenda listened to Adam's story, nodding and paying attention during parts when he expected her to be judgmental or critical. When he was finished talking, she told him about herself. Brenda was in her second year at Portland Community College. She wanted to be a nurse and was deeply involved in her church.

She looked at the water, and her eyes caught the reflection. "My dad's the pastor."

"Really?" Adam felt his eyes grow wide. Her dad was a pastor? He resisted the urge to back up, to run. He'd never spent this much time with a church girl, let alone one whose father was a minister.

"Mm-hmm." Her head fell back and she let out a light laugh. "Don't worry. He's not that bad."

Adam relaxed some. So what if her dad worked at church? She was the only girl he'd talked with since coming to the Northwest, and the glow in her eyes took his breath away. The conversation continued. "What's the name of your church?"

Brenda told him, and Adam could only stare at her, stunned. It was the same church Will and Wanda attended, the church they'd wanted him to visit for so long.

Adam and Brenda talked through the afternoon and attended the evening session with the speaker before saying good-bye. Adam wanted to ask her for her number, a way to see her again. But she seemed suddenly in a hurry, and they parted without a plan. That Saturday he visited Will and Wanda and told them about the girl.

"Oh, yes. Brenda. She's a beautiful girl." Will nodded. Then his eyes lit up. "I guess that means you'll have to come with us tomorrow."

Adam couldn't argue the point. The next day, dressed in his best jeans and T-shirt, he went to church. After the service he found Brenda outside chatting with a group of girls. She pulled herself away, and this time Adam didn't hesitate.

"I forgot something last time we were together."

"You did?" Her smile told him she knew what he was getting at.

"Yes. Can I have your number?"

Brenda hesitated, but only for a moment.

Their first date was that weekend, and they never looked back. But Adam refused to allow his relationship with her to be anything more than casual until he had a better understanding of God and everything a life with him meant. He attended Bible studies and one-on-one meetings with Will, and six months into his newly found faith, Brenda's father baptized Adam after a Sunday church service.

Will was the first to find him when it was over.

"I'm so happy for you." He winked. "How's that empty feeling?"

Adam smiled and the warmth of it went all the way through him. "It's gone." He hugged Will. "Thanks for praying for me, Will. Everything's different." He thought of Brenda. "Everything."

He and Brenda grew more serious over the next year, and at the two-year anniversary of their first meeting, Adam asked her to marry him. That week he wrote something in his journal that he looked at often: "I never knew I could feel like this, so complete and whole, so sure that everything is happening just as it should. I have the woman of my dreams at my side, and my best friend, Will Fredericks. Life couldn't be better."

For a long while things actually did get better.

Two years after Adam and Brenda married, Brenda learned she was going to have a baby. They celebrated by sharing dinner with Will and Wanda, and when the meal was over, Will pulled Adam aside in the living room. "Nothing in life beats having a baby." He pointed to the Bible on the end table. "Teach 'em the Good Word and everything'll turn out alright."

Adam appreciated the advice, and by the time Brenda was six months pregnant, they had a parenting plan. Will and Wanda were chosen as the baby's god-parents. By then, Adam and Brenda were meeting at the older couple's house once a week for Bible study, and the friendship between Adam and Will was stronger than ever.

"He's so many things to me," Adam explained to Brenda once. "Father, mentor, counselor." Adam paused. "But most of all, he's my friend. The best friend I've ever had."

"I'm glad." Brenda slipped her arms around his neck. "Friends like that are a gift from God."

At the time, neither Adam nor Brenda knew just how true those words would become.

Brenda's pregnancy went well for the next two months, but then, four weeks before her due date, she began to bleed. Adam rushed her to the hospital, and at first the good news came in a steady stream.

Doctors stabilized Brenda and delivered their baby, a boy who would be named William—after Adam's friend—and whom they would call Billy. Because of Brenda's emergency C-section, Adam wasn't allowed into the delivery room, but he was able to see little Billy a few minutes after he was born.

Adam touched the child's velvet-soft hand and prayed. *God, thank you for this miracle child. He's beautiful, and forever he will be a reminder to me of your faithfulness. Now, please . . . please let Brenda get better quickly because she needs to be here with us, enjoying this moment. And God, please let this child grow up to know you and—*

"Mr. Murphy?" The voice came from the doorway, breathless and panicked.

Adam turned around, and immediately he knew something was wrong. At the door was one of the doctors, his face pale and taut. With everything in him, Adam didn't want to ask, but he had no choice. He took three steps toward the man. "Is it Brenda?"

"Yes." The doctor's words were fast, anxious. "She started bleeding again. She's asking for you."

The next hour was a blur.

Adam followed the doctor to Brenda's hospital room, and there he found his wife awake, but almost too weak to talk. The doctors allowed him only a few seconds, so he took her hand, his eyes flashing from her to the doctors. What was this? What was happening? And why the serious overtones? They could stop bleeding, couldn't they? Wasn't that why she was at the hospital, so they could control the situation?

"Brenda, hang in there." Adam's heart raced as he

said the words. "Will called the church. Everyone's praying."

The doctor touched Adam's elbow. "I'm sorry. You'll have to leave. The situation is critical."

Adam squeezed Brenda's fingers and blew her a kiss. She only stared at him, a look of peace and knowing and fear all at once. Adam went to the waiting room and found Will, Brenda's parents, and a handful of church friends.

Will was on his feet first. "What is it, Adam?"

For a moment Adam couldn't speak. "She's...she's worse." He swallowed and leaned against the nearest wall. "Pray, please. Everyone."

And they did pray. For hours they prayed until finally the doctor returned. As soon as he walked into the room, Adam knew.

"I'm sorry." The doctor stared at the floor for a few seconds. "We did everything we could, but we lost her."

His words marked the beginning of a nightmare as dark as it was endless. From the beginning, Brenda's mother stepped in, offering to help care for the baby. After the second week Adam made a decision.

He took Billy to Brenda's parents' house and knocked on the door.

Brenda's mother answered. "Why, Adam...come in."

The couple had struggled much since Brenda's death, but they at least had a peace. A peace Adam no longer knew anything about. Adam handed Billy to Brenda's mother. "I can't take care of him. Would you..." Adam let his eyes fall to his newborn son. "Would you take him? I'll visit as often as I can but..." Tears choked his voice. Without Brenda, he had no idea how to get through a single day, let alone care for a baby. "I can't do it."

Brenda's mother took the baby, her mouth open, unspeaking. After a moment she nodded, and with her free hand she pulled Adam into a hug. "Get some help, Adam. Will would meet with you every day. You know that."

"I know." Adam stepped backwards a few feet. "I can't..." He shook his head. "I can't believe in a God who would..."

Neither of them said anything for a while. Then Brenda's mother wiped at the tears on her cheek and kissed Adam's forehead. "You need a few days, but you'll be back, Adam. God won't let you go that easily. Will's praying for you, and so am I."

Adam swallowed hard against the lump in his

throat. "Thank you." He took Billy's tiny fingers and held them against his cheek for a long moment. "Take care of him, okay?"

Then, without looking back, Adam turned and left.

Brenda's mother had been wrong about the timing, though. Adam stayed gone far longer than a few days. Though Will called and came by to see him, Adam couldn't pull himself from one undeniable truth: He'd prayed for Brenda, but still God had allowed her to die.

From the beginning he stopped attending the Bible study at Will and Wanda's house. And after a few months he packed his things into the back of his pickup truck and a U-Haul and moved north to Seattle. He left without saying good-bye to Brenda's parents, Will and Wanda, or even little Billy.

Another year passed, and Adam had trouble finding work. He couldn't concentrate through an entire eight-hour shift, couldn't focus on fixing radiators and tuning engines with the love of his life dead and buried. Worse, Billy was growing up without his daddy, but Adam felt too overcome with grief to change the situation.

At the beginning of his second year in Seattle,

Adam was evicted from his apartment for non-payment. He was out of money, out of options, and desperate for answers. More than once, he'd take a meal at the downtown mission where someone would talk to him about God or church. Always the idea made him sick with anger. He would not believe in a God who could take Brenda, could not fathom stepping foot in a church, and wouldn't stand for anyone to talk to him about prayer.

Instead, he wanted only to die, to find a way to join Brenda.

That week, he made a plan. He would scrounge up enough money to buy a gun, go back to Portland, and say good-bye to Billy. Then he'd hold up a store and wait until someone shot him. It was a desperate idea, but Adam couldn't think of any other way.

He still had his pickup, so he drove south on Interstate 5 until he reached Vancouver, Washington—just ten miles north of Portland. He had only a few miles before he ran out of gas. He pulled off at a rest stop and searched his entire car—his wallet, glove box, floorboards, even underneath the seats—but all he found was forty-three cents.

Desperate to see Billy before enacting his plan, Adam made a decision. He would rob the first convenience store he saw in Vancouver, take enough money to buy gas, then carry out his steps the way he'd planned them. He took an exit in northern Vancouver and headed for the first mini-mart gas station he saw.

Sweat beaded up on his forehead as he headed for the front door. In his pocket was a loaded revolver. Okay, he thought to himself. This is it. Get a little cash quick and get out of here. The last thing he wanted was to use the gun or have someone hurt him before he had a chance to say good-bye to his son.

He walked through the front door and quickly toward the cashier. A glance over his shoulder told him the store was empty other than the man behind the counter, who was watching something on a small overhead television. Adam poked the tip of his gun through his jacket pocket and was about to order the man to hand over the cash in the register when he heard something behind him.

"Adam!" The voice was old and scratchy. "I can't believe it's you!"

Adam's hands shook. Who would know him here, after so long away from the area? He spun around, the gun still poking through his pocket. "What do you w—"

And at that instant, Adam's hand went limp. The man standing before him was Will Fredericks. He looked older, a little more stooped. But his eyes had the same bright glow as before. "Adam, it's been too long."

Adam took a step back, trembling from the emotions raging in his heart. Part of him wanted to yell at his old friend, tell him to leave so he could finish what he'd come to do. But if Will knew what Adam was up to, he didn't let on. Instead he reached out and set his hand on Adam's shoulder. "I hope this means you're coming home."

Then and there, with the cashier staring strangely at them, Adam began to cry. Will led him outside and they both climbed into Will's pickup. The crying became weeping, the sort of grief-stricken sobbing Adam hadn't done since losing Brenda. He covered his face with his hands and sniffed. "Everyone expected me to move on after losing her, and I couldn't. I could barely remember how to walk, let alone live without her."

Will listened for almost an hour, then he offered to pray. At that point, Adam held his hand up. "Me and God are done."

"You are, huh?" Will managed a sad smile. "Well, we'll see about that."

They talked a while longer, and at the end Will gave Adam his trademark wink. "I think I'll put some gas in your car so you can follow me home."

"Follow you?"

"Yes. As soon as I saw you, I felt God tell me you needed a place. Maybe for a few nights."

Adam could do nothing but nod his head.

That night was the beginning of a string of events Adam couldn't come close to explaining. How could he have been back in the Portland-Vancouver area for less than an hour and run smack into Will Fredericks? How could Will have known about the empty gas tank? And how could this all have happened on the very night Adam had planned on killing himself?

The memories faded and Adam glanced at Will sitting beside him in the church pew.

Never once had Will done anything but love him. He'd helped Adam to see his son and watched as Adam held him for the first time since he was a newborn. And that, finally, was what had led Adam to this place—sitting beside his old friend in the pew of a church he'd vowed to never set foot in again.

He heard something behind him and turned around. There was Brenda's mother, walking a toddling little Billy down the aisle. Adam watched them, his eyes teary. They'd talked and Brenda's mother had agreed that gradually—as Adam found a job and stability—Billy would go back to him. For now, Brenda's mother also had tears in her eyes.

Tears of joy.

She slid in beside Adam, hugged him, and placed Billy on his lap. "I still can't believe you're here," she whispered to him.

Adam nodded and he wondered where he'd be right now if God hadn't sent Will into the store that fateful night. Dead, most likely. Or in jail with a pending trial. He would've lost Billy forever. Billy, who had Brenda's eyes and smile.

Adam shuddered and glanced at Will. "It's a miracle I'm here. Thank you. Thank you for everything."

Will's eyes lit up. He leaned close and whispered something that made Adam feel loved and trusted and valuable all at once, something he remembers to this day: "You're my friend, Adam. I asked God to help me out with you, and that's what he did. It's his miracle, not mine."

To Run, to Fly

Steven Sanders and Jimmy Rowden grew up next door to each other in a suburb of Chicago. They were buddies before they were old enough to walk and fast friends by the time kindergarten arrived. Mornings were spent at school and afternoons at one of their houses, building snowball forts or, when spring came, pretending they were the Cubs, and their adjoining backyards, Wrigley Field.

They had something else in common. They were both being raised in broken homes, in which their mothers were busy working two jobs and a babysitter was the closest thing to adult attention they had in the afternoons and evenings.

"Those two need each other," Steven heard another neighbor comment once. "I can't imagine how they'd get along if they were separated."

The boys' friendship wasn't just a matter of convenience and location. They both dreamed high, and by the time they reached third grade, Steven was sure he wanted to fly when he was older.

"I'll be the best pilot in the world," he told Jimmy on one of their summer bike rides around the neighborhood. "Up there in the air, it'll be the best feeling in the world."

Jimmy also had a dream. He was the fastest boy in his class, a few inches taller than Steven. He wanted to be a runner in the Olympics one day, maybe even the fastest man in the world.

"Everyone'll know my name," he'd say as he'd thump his chest, then giggle the way little boys do when their dreams are big. "I'll win a heap o' gold medals and then I'll retire and go fishing."

The trouble with Steven's and Jimmy's dreams was that no one in their lives thought they were attainable. Especially not their mothers.

"Don't go expecting to be a pilot," Steven's mother would tell him. "Flying planes is a rich person's hobby. And we'll never be rich people." She'd give him a distracted smile. "Think about working down at the factory like your grandpa. That's a real job, Steven."

Jimmy's mother was equally discouraging. "Running isn't something serious," she said as often as the subject came up. "You can't be a kid forever, Jimmy."

The boys talked about their mothers' feelings and agreed that their lack of enthusiasm only made them want their dreams more. Sometimes they'd run through the fields adjacent to their neighborhood—Steven with his hands outstretched like wings, and Jimmy covering the ground as fast as the wind. While they ran they'd shout back and forth, loud enough for people in the neighboring houses to hear.

"I want to fly!" Steven would dip one arm and raise the other in a tight turn.

Then it would be Jimmy's turn. "I want to run!"

"I want to fly!"

"I want to run!"

Never mind about their mothers. Steven and Jimmy believed nothing in all of existence could stop them from reaching their goals.

But all that changed the summer before fifth grade.

One hot Wednesday in August, Jimmy's dad picked him up for a day at a local lake with his cousins. Jimmy rarely spent time with his dad, so he'd been looking forward to the day for weeks. The lake had a pier in the middle of a roped-off swimming area, a wooden platform covered with kids jumping off.

"No diving, okay?" His father popped open a drink and dug his beach chair into the sand. "And look out for your cousins."

Jimmy and his three cousins, each about the same age as him, headed for the water. In no time they swam out to the pier where a jumping contest turned into a game of tag. Jimmy, always quicker than the others, played game after game without being caught. The four boys were taking a minute to catch their breath when Jimmy's cousins grinned and whispered something to each other.

"Your turn to get it, Jimmy," one of them shouted, and then amidst peals of laughter and bursts of motion, they ran toward him.

"Oh, no, you're not." Jimmy raised his fist in the air. "No one catches me!" They were going for his shoulder, and Jimmy knew it. Forgetting his father's warning, he pushed off the edge of the pier and dove into the shallow water.

For a single moment, Jimmy rejoiced at escaping their touch, at still being the only boy who hadn't been tagged. But the very next second, his head hit the lake bottom and he felt a crushing, burning feeling in his spine. He started to scream for help, but he couldn't find the breath, couldn't kick, couldn't make himself rise to the surface for air. Couldn't do anything but hope his cousins could see the obvious.

If someone didn't help him, he was going to drown.

Steven didn't know something was wrong until two days later. Jimmy should've been home from his trip with his father, but Steven hadn't seen a sign of him or his mother. Finally he went to Jimmy's door, knocked, and waited. An old woman answered the door, someone Steven had never seen before.

"Can I help you?" Her eyes were red and swollen.

"Uh, yes, ma'am. Is Jimmy home?"

The woman covered her mouth with one hand and shook her head. Then she swallowed hard and closed her eyes. "He's been hurt." She blinked, and her eyes looked sadder than anything Steven had seen. "I'm his grandma."

"Hurt?" A heaviness settled over Steven's chest. "How'd he get hurt?"

And then the old woman told him.

Jimmy had broken his neck diving into the lake bottom. The fastest runner at Wright Elementary School would never run again. Jimmy was paralyzed from the waist down, and though Steven didn't understand the medical term, he understood when Jimmy came home from the hospital.

Steven stood outside on the corner of his yard and watched in horror as Jimmy's mother and grandmother pulled a wheelchair from the back of their car, spread out the wheels and the seat, and lifted Jimmy into it. From the distant place where he watched, he wasn't sure what to do, how to help. But he was sure of one thing—a wheelchair wasn't going to get in the way of his friendship with Jimmy Rowden.

For three straight days after Jimmy's mother went to work, his grandma wheeled him out onto his front porch. On the fourth day, Steven was waiting. The boys waited until the old woman was back in the house. Then Steven leaned against the porch rail and looked at his feet, not sure what to say.

Finally Jimmy broke the silence. "I still want to run."

Steven looked at his friend. He could feel tears in his eyes, but he didn't want to cry. So he walked up to Jimmy's wheelchair, put his arm around his friend's shoulders, and said, "I still want to fly."

Over the next few weeks, Steven became more comfortable with Jimmy's paralysis. The two found their way around Jimmy's handicap, tossing a football back and forth, fishing at the lake, and still spending more of their free time together than apart.

One day they were in Jimmy's front yard feeling bored when Steven had an idea. "Let's go to the field and play!"

Jimmy's smile faded. "I can't."

"Why not?" Steven wanted Jimmy to do everything he used to do.

"Because." Frustration sounded in Jimmy's voice. He breathed a heavy sigh. "You know how bad my chair does in the dirt."

"Oh." Steven thought about that for a moment. "Wait! We can go to the abandoned road, the one on the other side of the field. Your chair can go there."

Doubt clouded Jimmy's eyes. "How'll I get there?"

"That's easy." Steven flexed his arms and grinned at his friend. "I'll push you."

Steven wheeled Jimmy and his chair down the street, along a sidewalk near the empty field, and into a stretch of dead-end roadway. For a moment they stood there, silent. This was the place where their dreams had always felt most possible. But here, now, with Jimmy in a wheelchair, they seemed all but dead.

Jimmy looked at Steven. "Think I'll ever walk again?"

"Sure." Steven's answer was quick. "I'll help you. That ol' chair is just for now, until your legs get better."

Jimmy nodded and stared at the sea of wild grass on the adjacent field. The sun was hidden behind the clouds, and a chill wind blew down the empty street. Jimmy turned to Steven. "Think I'll ever run again?"

The question seemed almost laughable. Jimmy Rowden? Of course he'd run again, right? But the truth was something altogether different, and even as a young boy, Steven knew better than to say yes. But just then, with the certainties of tomorrow looming more empty than the open field, Steven had a thought.

"Hey." He turned and stared at Jimmy. "Maybe we can have our dream today, right here!"

Jimmy twisted his brow. He put his hands on the wheels of his chair and moved it back a bit. "What dream?"

"You know..." Steven pointed to the sky. "Me flying and you running."

Before Jimmy could say anything, Steven ran behind his wheelchair and began pushing it. Faster and faster he went, straight down the long, dead-end road. When he'd picked up enough speed, he jumped up and placed his feet on a bar that ran along the back of the chair. Then, leaning his body forward against Jimmy's back, Steven held out both arms and laughed out loud. "Look, Jimmy!"

His friend turned his head enough to see. "Steven, you're crazy." Jimmy didn't sound confused anymore. A familiar easy smile filled his face. "What're you doing?"

"Can't you see?" Steven let out a loud hoot and let his head fall back, arms still outstretched. "I'm flying, Jimmy. I'm really flying!"

When the wheelchair came to a stop, Steven hopped down, breathless. "Okay," he walked around to the front of Jimmy's chair. "Now it's your turn."

"Wha—"

Jimmy couldn't even get his question out before Steven stooped down, pulled Jimmy's limp legs around his own waist, and shouted, "Hold on!"

"Really?" Jimmy looped his arms around Steven's neck.

"Really." Steven bounced a few times to shift Jimmy up. With his friend balanced in piggy-back style, Steven took off running back down the street. Faster and faster he ran, and from behind him he could hear Jimmy's laughter mixing with the wind.

"I'm running! You're right, Steven! I'm running again!"

Indeed, in that moment their dreams felt as real as life itself.

But the years passed and still Jimmy did not learn to walk again. The friends began praying to God, asking him that one day Steven might learn to fly and Jimmy might find his way to the Olympics.

Everything about their friendship came to a halt in seventh grade, the year Jimmy and his mother moved to California.

"I'll write," Jimmy promised the day before he left. "We'll always be friends. And whatever we do, let's promise to pray about our dreams."

And at first the two boys did write. But over time the letters slowed and eventually stopped. What didn't stop was their determination to pray about their dreams. Despite physical and financial limitations, Jimmy wanted to be in the Olympics and Steven wanted to fly. And though they were no longer in contact they continued to pray and pursue their goals.

Seventeen years passed, and Steven worked his way through the Air Force Academy and into a job as a commercial pilot. Often when he took to the skies he would thank God for letting his dream come true—flying was everything he'd hoped it would be. But he also wondered about Jimmy, whether doctors were ever able to help him walk again, and even more—whether he had learned to run.

One winter morning Steven had more time than usual after his flight preparations. He nodded to his copilot and motioned toward the cabin. "I'll be back. I wanna check out the cabin."

He made his way down the center aisle, smiling and making eye contact with passengers. When he had time, Steven loved to see the people he'd be flying; their faces made him realize the awesome responsibility of taking so many people into the air. He was almost to the back of the plane when he spotted a man who looked familiar.

Steven needed only a few seconds before his breath caught in his throat. He walked up to the man and cocked his head. "Jimmy Rowden?"

The passenger's eyes fell to the gold name plate and the word *Sanders* on Steven's uniform. His eyes grew wide. "Steven?"

"I can't believe it's you! I figured I'd never see you again."

Jimmy shook his head, his eyes damp. "This is too strange."

Right there, with passengers filling the seats, the two men clasped hands.

"You got your dream, man! Look at you, flying this big ol' plane."

They talked about their families—both were married with two children—then the conversation stalled. All Steven could think about was whether Jimmy had gotten the use of his legs back. He opened his mouth to ask his long-ago friend whether he'd gotten his dream, whether he was running or not. But at that moment he spotted a pair of short crutches lying against the empty seat beside Jimmy and a sudden fear seized his heart. If Jimmy still had crutches...

His old friend made a small coughing sound and then grabbed the crutches and swung himself up to his feet. He gave Steven a hard hug and a friendly pounding on his back. "Did you pray for me?"

"Yes." Steven struggled to find his voice. Why hadn't God healed his friend, given him back the use of his legs? "Yes, I prayed for you all the time. I still do."

"Me, too." Jimmy shrugged, a smile stretching across his face. "So I guess God heard both our prayers."

Steven didn't know what to say. "What..." He couldn't ask, couldn't look Jimmy in the eyes after so much time and question whether he'd really gotten his dream or not.

Almost as if he was guessing Steven's thoughts, Jimmy laughed. "Guess where I'm flying to?"

"Where?" Steven kept his voice lower than before. The passengers were almost completely seated and he'd have to take the cockpit in a few minutes.

Jimmy held his arms out, his eyes dancing. "The qualifying meet for the Olympics, man! I've been working on it for a few years now, and I'm a long shot for the 100-yard!"

"The Olympics?" Steven didn't want to stare, but he caught himself glancing at Jimmy's crutches.

"The Wheelchair Olympics!" Jimmy leaned against the side of his seat cushion and shook his head. "I still wanna run, and this feels almost the way it did back when I still could. Right before you came down the aisle, I was thinking about that, remembering how we'd take that field shouting, 'I want to run!'"

"I want to fly."

"And now..." He tossed his hands in the air and gave Steven another hug. "Here we are!"

Steven thought of the odds that he and Jimmy would wind up on the same plane, on the day Jimmy was headed off for the Olympics. A chill passed over him. "You're right." He narrowed his eyes, awed at the way things had worked out. "God did hear our prayers. It's a miracle, after all."

Note: *After reconnecting at that chance meeting on the plane, Steven and Jimmy stayed friends. Jimmy survived the qualifying heat at the Wheelchair Olympics. A few months later, he won gold at the Wheelchair Olympics. Steven flew out to watch the race.*

#1 *New York Times* Author
Karen Kingsbury

www.KarenKingsbury.com

More Books in the Miracles Series by Karen Kingsbury

#1 *New York Times* Bestselling Author

A TREASURY OF MIRACLES FOR WOMEN

Heartwarming true stories show God at work in the lives of mothers, sisters, wives, and friends.

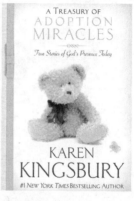

A TREASURY OF ADOPTION MIRACLES

Inspiring true stories that illuminate God's miraculous presence in adoption.

A TREASURY OF MIRACLES FOR TEENS

Amazing real life stories especially for and about teens that illustrate how God is nearest in the most challenging of times.

And look for the Red Gloves Series

GIDEON'S GIFT

Seven-year-old Gideon suffers from leukemia but still believes with all her heart that "Christmas means never having to ask God how much he loves us." Will she be able to convince Earl, a homeless man hardened by personal tragedy, of the miracle of Christmas—and perhaps receive a miracle of her own?

SARAH'S SONG

Sarah Lindman is a resident at the Greer Retirement Village in South Carolina who celebrates Christmas the same special way each year. This time, she'll share her ornament and song ritual with a young nurse in need of the healing power it brings.

HANNAH'S HOPE

At fifteen years old, Hannah Roberts is shocked to learn a life-changing secret about her identity. Only a Christmas miracle can reunite the girl with her father when he goes missing on an Air Force assignment.

MAGGIE'S MIRACLE

High-powered attorney Maggie Wright no longer believes in romance, not since she was a starry-eyed teen. But a chance meeting could uncover what she thought was lost to her past, including her faith in love.

Available now in print and ebook formats from FaithWords wherever books are sold.

Turn the page for an
excerpt from
Karen Kingsbury's

Maggie's
Miracle

The letter was his best idea yet.

Jordan Wright had already talked to God about getting his wish, and so far nothing had happened. But a letter...a letter would definitely get God's attention. Not the crayoned pictures he liked to send Grandpa in California. But a real letter. On his mom's fancy paper with his best spelling and slow hands, so his a's and e's would sit straight on the line the way a second grader's a's and e's should.

That way, God would read it for sure.

Grandma Terri was watching her yucky grown-up show on TV. People kissing and crying and yelling at each other. Every day his grandma picked him up from St. Andrews, brought him home to their Upper East Side apartment in Manhattan, got him a snack, and put in the video of her grown-up show. Jordan could make his own milk shakes or accidentally color on the walls or jump on his bed for an hour when Grandma watched her grown-up show. As long as he wasn't too loud, she didn't notice anything.

"This is my time, Jordan," she'd tell him, and her eyes would get that in-charge kind of look. "Keep yourself busy."

But when the show was over she'd find him and make a loud, huffy sound. "Jordan," she'd say, "what are you into now? Why can't you read quietly like other children?" Her voice would be slow and tired, and Jordan wouldn't know what to do next.

She never yelled at him or sent him to his room, but one thing was sure. She didn't like baby-sitting him because yesterday Jordan heard her tell his mom that.

"I can't handle the boy forever, Megan. It's been two years since George died. You need a nanny." She did a different kind of breathy noise. "The boy's wearing me out."

Jordan had been in his room listening. He felt bad because maybe it was his fault his grandma couldn't handle him. But then he heard his mom say, "I can't handle him, either, so that makes two of us."

After that Jordan felt too sick to eat dinner.

Ever since then he'd known it was time. He had to do whatever it took to get God's attention because if he didn't get his wish pretty soon, well, maybe his mom and his grandma might not like him anymore.

It wasn't that he tried to get into trouble. But some-times it was boring looking for things to do, and he'd get curious and wonder what would happen if he made a milk shake with ice cubes. But how was he supposed to know the milk-shake maker had a lid? And using paper and a red crayon to trace the tiger on the wall calendar probably wasn't a good idea in the first place, because of course sometimes crayons slip.

He took the last swallow from his milk and waited until the cookie crumbs slid down the glass into his mouth. Cookies were the best snack of all. He set the cup on the counter, climbed off the barstool, and walked with tiptoe feet into his mom's office. He wasn't allowed in there except if his mom was work-ing on her lawyer stuff and he had to ask her a serious question.

But she'd understand today because a letter to God was very serious business.

The room was big and clean and full of wood stuff. His mom was the kind of lawyer who put bad guys in jail. That's why sometimes she had to work late at night and on Sundays. Jordan pulled open a drawer near his mother's computer and took out two pieces of paper and two envelopes, in case he messed up and had to start over. Then he snuck real quiet out the door, down the hall, and into his room. He had a desk and pencils in there, only he never used them because second graders at St. Andrews didn't get homework till after Christmas.

One time he asked his mommy what would happen if he couldn't do the homework when he got it, what if the stuff he had to do was too hard.

"It won't be too hard, Jordan." His mother's eyebrows had lifted up the way they did when she didn't want any more questions.

"Are you sure?"

"Yes, I'm completely sure."

"How come?"

"Because, Jordan, I've been through second grade and I know all the answers. If you have trouble, I'll help you."

His heart felt a little less scared after that. Not every second grader's mommy had *all* the answers. If she knew everything, then he could never really get in too much trouble with his homework, and that was a good thing because Christmas wasn't too far away.

He sat down at his desk, took a pencil from the box, and spread out the piece of paper. The white space looked very empty. Jordan stared at it for a long time. If God was going to read the letter, it had to be his best work ever. Big words would be a good thing. He worked himself a little taller in the chair, sucked in a long breath through his teeth, and began to write.

Dear God, my name is Jordan Wright and I am 8 years old. I hav somthing to ask you. I tride to ask you befor but I think you wer bizy. So I am riting you a letter insted.

Jordan's hand hurt by the time he finished, and he could hear music playing on Grandma's grown-up show. That meant it was almost done, and any minute Grandma would come looking for him. He quickly folded the letter in half, ran his finger along the edge, and folded it again. Then he stuck it in the envelope and licked the lid shut. With careful fingers he wrote "God" across the front, then his pencil moved down a bit and froze. He'd forgotten something.

He didn't know God's address.

His heart felt extra jumpy. God lived in heaven, so that had to be part of it. But what about the numbers?

Jordan could hear footsteps coming closer. He didn't want Grandma to see the letter. She might want to read it, and that would ruin everything because it was a secret. Just between him and God. He looked around his room and saw his backpack near his bed. He ran fast to it and slipped the letter inside. He could give it to his mother on the way to school tomorrow. She would know God's address.

She knew everything.